TAUGHT TO SERVE

Taught to Serve

The History of the
Barry and Bryntirion Colleges

Noel Gibbard

EVANGELICAL PRESS OF WALES

© Evangelical Press of Wales, 1996
First published 1996
ISBN 1 85049 122 4

Cover design:
Rhiain M. Davies (Cain)
Cover photographs:
B. S. Fidler, John Waite and Eryl Davies

Published by Evangelical Press of Wales
Bryntirion, Bridgend, Mid Glamorgan
CF31 4DX, Wales, UK
Printed in Wales by D. Brown & Sons Ltd.
Bridgend

Contents

Illustrations

Preface

The little word 'remember' appears often in the Scriptures. It is a word that we should not forget. There is a need for us to be continually reminded of the faithfulness and goodness of God. There is no doubt that the good hand of the Lord has been upon the College at Barry and Bryntirion, and as we remember the past sixty years, may our hearts be drawn out to truly praise our God. During the whole of that period his mercies have not failed.

The work started at Barry in 1936, but it is essential to go beyond that date in order to follow the story meaningfully. Consequently, the first chapter traces the background in general terms, shows how Barry emerged from Porth, and establishes the role played by the Rev. B. S. Fidler in the events leading to the formation of the School for Evangelism in Barry.

The number of people who have helped with the preparation of the book is legion. I would like to thank all of those who have contributed in any way, by letter, telephone call, conversation or by sending photographs. There are some who have provided me with important source material, and I gratefully acknowledge their help: Revs Stanley Jackson, Thorpe, Essex; Ken Peel, Yeovil; Norman Lloyd, Cheltenham; David Carey-Jones, Llangeinor; Mr Maurice Caughey, Talbot Green; Mrs McHaffie, Bristol, and Mrs Baggs,

Barry. Mrs M. Selway, Cardiff, provided me with valuable information on a number of occasions. She was always at hand whenever I had a problem in identifying a student, and it is quite remarkable how she keeps in touch with so many past students. Mrs Menna Bowen, Cardiff, daughter of the Rev. R. B. Jones, kindly gave me permission to quote from her father's correspondence, as did Dr Stephen Nantlais Williams, Belfast, to quote from the letters of his grandfather, the Rev. Nantlais Williams.

Dr Eryl Davies and Mr Clem Roberts, MA, read parts of the work and made valuable suggestions. The list would not be complete without acknowledging the careful and thorough work of Miss Mair Jones and Mr Edmund Owen in preparing the volume for the press.

April 1996   NOEL GIBBARD

1.
Pioneering at Porth
1916–1936

On 31 August 1916, the minister of a Baptist church, in Porth, Rhondda, was presiding over a meeting during which he said farewell to an African Inland Mission worker.[1] The event is significant in many respects. The pastor was the Rev. R. B. Jones (1869–1933), a leading figure in evangelical circles and a central Welsh link with prominent developments in Britain, in terms of the Revival of 1904–05, the Holiness Movement and Faith Missions. It was in his home in the Rhondda valley that the 'Alquin Club' met during May 1903 to pray for personal spiritual renewal and revival.[2] This group contacted the Rev. F. B. Meyer, a leading exponent of the Keswick teaching and a staunch advocate of Faith missions. He encouraged them to go to the first Keswick in Wales at Llandrindod in August, and there they met Meyer himself, Mrs Penn-Lewis, Rhys Davies and others.

During that same period, 1903–04, ministers of the Presbyterian Church in Wales were concerned with the spiritual condition of the land, and meetings were held in West Wales to intercede for an awakening. In one of those meetings, when Seth Joshua (1858–1925), of the Forward Movement, prayed, 'Bend us', Evan Roberts experienced what he described as his Gethsemane.[3] In the heat of this experience he returned to his home village, Loughor, West Glamorgan, ready to travel the country with the mighty hand of God upon him.

Included in the group of speakers at the West Wales conventions were W. S. Jones (1860–1933) (Baptist), W. W. Lewis (1856–1938), (Calvinistic Methodist), and Keri Evans (1860–1941), (Congregationalist), the three of them ministering in Carmarthen.[4] W. S. Jones had experienced a deepening of his spiritual life on at least two remarkable occasions, during his stay in America, and shortly after returning. He influenced the other two and both of them, Lewis and Keri Evans, were also indebted to Reader Harris of the Pentecostal League. The other factor which led Keri Evans into his crisis experience was the visit to Carmarthen of Mrs Penn-Lewis and the Rev. R. B. Jones, Porth, who was being used mightily in the Revival.[5] All of them would describe their experience as being filled with the Holy Spirit. W. S. Jones moved to Rhondda and a closer friendship was established between the two Joneses. Another person who moved to the same valley was Sidney Evans (1884–1960), who married Evan Roberts' sister, and W. W. Lewis, Keri Evans and Seth Joshua were to be regular visitors to Porth. The last mentioned was one with the others in their emphasis on revival, but more critical than they were of the Keswick movement.

The burden of revival never left R. B. Jones, and he did everything possible to keep alive the experiences of the past, but also found means to strengthen and renew the experiences of the believers. With others, he brought out *Yr Efengylydd* (The Evangelist), whose aims were, 'To keep alive the spirit of the revival, to spread the truths emphasized by the revival, and to build up the faith and holiness of people blessed by the revival'.[6] Another means of teaching the believers and deepen their spiritual lives was to hold conventions, locally, as well as at Llandrindod. R. B. Jones worked with the Rev. Nantlais Williams, Ammanford (1874–1959), and others to arrange these meetings, aiming, (1) to Unite the children of the Revival across denominational barriers, (2) Deepen giving; be more liberal, and, (3) With Wesley say, 'The world is my parish'.[7] Christians should not only meet to edify each other but they should be willing to take the gospel to others, at home and abroad. Wales was part of the parish, and R. B. Jones, W. S. Jones, W. W. Lewis, O. M. Owen and Keri Evans were always available to travel the country. As far as they were concerned evangelism was a must. These developments led to more aggressive evangelism by the formation of the Faith Mission of Wales. 'For years, its readers [*Yr Efengylydd*], supported missioners, who, using a portable wooden tent in winter, and a caravan in summer (both the gifts of the readers), toured the Principality seeking the lost.'[8]

Evangelism at home and mission work overseas were two sides of the same coin. R. B. Jones did not neglect either aspect. He worked untiringly at home, was full of enthusiasm to promote the witness in other countries, and welcomed wholeheartedly the emergence of new faith missionary societies. The need in other lands was brought home forcefully to him at that valedictory service on 31 August 1916. His feelings at the time are revealed by one of his friends, 'His deepest desire was that his Church might become a missionary one in the true sense of the word.'[9]

The enemy attacks

However, if men and women were to take the gospel to different parts of Wales and other countries, how could they be prepared for such a task? Marked changes were taking place in Wales, the Revival of '04 was even ridiculed, and some of the central truths of the gospel were being denied, although, generally speaking, the congregations were ortho-dox, thanks to some faithful ministers, the impact of the Revival, the Sunday school and the hymn-books. There were signs of changes even before the end of the nineteenth century, the authorship of the Penta-teuch being an issue during the 1890s, followed by a consideration of the composition of the Book of Psalms and the Unity of Isaiah.[10] Higher critical prin-ciples were creeping into Wales, preparing the way for more revolutionary changes. Dr R. Tudur Jones, with his usual, clear insight, summarizes the situ-ation:[11]

Generally speaking, as the field is surveyed, it must be said that until 1914 the radical Higher Critics had not gained much ground in Wales. The weight of Welsh opinion was on the conservative side. However, the champions of Higher Criticism were gaining ground in the colleges, and when the full tide of their influence was felt on ministers, there was a strong re-action against conservative views from 1914 onwards.

The seed had been sown and it was to reap a devas-tating harvest.

Those who were the leaders in these new developments were prepared in colleges in England, Scotland and Germany, not forgetting the Presbyterian College in Carmarthen, where Vance Smith was referred to as 'ad-Vance Smith', because of his critical attitude to Scripture and the orthodox faith.[12] The tradition was continued by Philemon Moore and J. Oliver Stephens. The latter paid a funeral tribute to the Unitarian principal of the College, and rejoiced that, 'He has gone to be with his beloved Plato.'[13] His words were an echo of Origen and a pointer to John Hick.

Vance Smith and others were influenced by developments in biblical criticism, theology and philosophy. In the context of biblical criticism the Bible was considered as any other book and the development of the religion of Israel as the development of any other religion, except that it reached a higher level in the teaching of the prophets. Theologically, God was the God of order and natural laws. He would not intervene in the course of history, and miracles were unacceptable. God never asked for atonement for sin, and his wrath must be understood in terms of cause and effect, not in personal terms as coming from God himself.

In the realm of philosophy idealism was the fashionable teaching under the influence of Hegelianism. This philosophy strongly emphasized the immanence of God and how He was present in all created things, Christ being the highest example of that truth. One author, commenting on the positive contribution of immanentists, the attack on deism and the generosity of spirit, added his opinion,

'Having allowed all this, we cannot overlook the fact that all types of immanentism really look to man—to his reason, his conscience or his religious experience—as the arbiter of truth.'[14] Three clear developments emerge: the acceptance of the principles of evolution—what was accepted in science was now applied to religion; the Bible could no longer be accepted as infallible and inspired; and, lastly, the need of the day was to concentrate on social issues rather than on personal salvation.

The developments were deeply rooted in Germany but sprang up in many places in Britain, especially in Oxford and Glasgow. In Oxford changes in biblical criticism were accepted by T. K. Cheyne and Buchanan Grey, theological changes welcomed by A. M. Fairbairn (1838–1912), while the most influential representative of idealism was Edward Caird, who had also spent some time in Glasgow. His teaching was represented in Wales by Henry Jones (1852–1922), who studied under Caird, and David Adams (1845–1923). Fairbairn remained supreme in Mansfield College, Oxford, from 1886 until 1909. During that period a number of men from Wales were educated at the College, including E. O. Davies (CM) Herbert Morgan (B), brought up in Salem, Porth, Thomas Rees, J. Morgan Jones and Miall Edwards (Cong.). E. O. Davies went on to receive further education in four German universities, Herbert Morgan entered Marburg, as did Thomas Lewis (Cong.), and D. F. Roberts (CM). J. Morgan Jones went to Berlin where he found a hero in Harnack, J. T. Evans (B) chose Leipzig and Joseph Jones (Cong.) decided on Heidelberg.

All these men became most influential in pulpit and college. For example, Joseph Jones was a lecturer at Brecon College from 1907 until 1943, when he was made Principal. Thomas Rees was Principal of Bala-Bangor College, Bangor, from 1909 until 1926, followed by J. Morgan Jones.[15] The link with the University of Wales provided another channel for the influence of the new ideas to reach the people of Wales. Once the old guard died, men like William Edwards (B), Lewis Probert (Cong.), and Cynddylan Jones (CM), the champions of evangelicalism became a small minority, and some of those became further removed from the historic denominations, while others aligned themselves with different Pentecostal groupings.

Marshalling the forces

This moving away from denominational commitment had already happened in England. The Keswick Convention attracted the crowds from across denominational boundaries, and the China Inland Mission under Hudson Taylor, one of the founders of Keswick, became the forerunner of many similar societies. These societies made evangelism central, worked on the faith principle, welcomed male and female workers, regarded church matters as secondary and, eschatologically, were premillennialist. Unity was thought of in terms of individuals and not in terms of churches.

Eschatologically, the teaching of the leaders, and in many cases that of the missionary societies, officially, was that of premillennialism. R. B. Jones was

a tenacious champion of the view. He was grieved
that only a few men accepted the view before the Revival of 1904, but with the awakening many people
received the new light. 'To the writer, as well as to
many others, a most striking feature of the work was
the light that came with it upon the truth of the pre-
millennial, personal advent of our Lord', which R. B.
Jones believed was 'a most remarkable fact'.[16]

This view was important for a number of reasons.
First of all, it had a charismatic significance. Believers were being taught by the Holy Spirit, and had
come to a common mind concerning this particular
truth. What was true of the pastor of Tabernacle,
Porth, was true of many others: 'Never can he forget
the occasion, the place, nor the day when, alone with
God, the truth flashed into his heart.'[17] Secondly, the
belief demanded a literal interpretation of Scripture,
which was, very often, dogmatically adhered to,
other views looked upon as being unsound. Thirdly,
it had a missionary significance, often related to
dispensationalist teaching. The reign of Christ was
being realized in the present, but there was a need to
hasten that process so that a great number of believers would be taken up at the rapture, immediately
before the personal return of Christ, who would rule
for a thousand years, and then usher in the day of
judgment for unbelievers. Believers could hasten
that day of Christ's coming by being faithful or pro-
long it by being unfaithful (2 Peter 3:12).[18]

The growth of the Christian Missionary Alliance
illustrates the impact this teaching could have on a
group of people: 'During 1891–1900, CMA experienced an unparalleled "missionary explosion", and

Simpson's eschatology of expecting Christ not at any moment but when the church has done her duty, is one of the explanations as to why it took place.'[19] There was an urgency to evangelize, and when Hudson Taylor accepted the teaching, he gave away everything which he thought was unnecessary for his work. C. T. Studd was of the same mind, and R. B. Jones was in that tradition. Their belief, as Klaus Fiedler would say, was 'applied eschatology'.[20]

Lastly, the conviction tended to keep the believer's attention on the future, and in such a way that he would disregard social and political issues. It gave men, including R. B. Jones, a weapon with which to fight the modernist, with his emphasis on the kingdom of heaven on earth. To make use of words spoken later by Dr Soper, the new evangelicalism aimed for the 'pie in the sky', while the advancing modernist claimed 'ham where I am'. The older evangelicalism had endeavoured to give priority to the personal, but also made an effort to apply scriptural principles to society. It is so easy to have an imbalance, either way. The prominent exception in the fundamentalist tradition was F. B. Meyer who was socially active.[21] Not all the evangelical leaders in Wales would be happy with the label 'fundamentalist', but R. B. Jones was quite happy to be dubbed as such. With him, as with some others, there was a tendency to anti-intellectualism, oppositionalism and a counter-culture emphasis, or, a 'ghetto mentality'.[22] While remaining officially within the Baptist Union he became less and less involved in its activities. Separatism was not carried to such extremes in Wales as in America, and there was less in-fighting than in that country. The Mission Halls, however, were committed to a strict 'come outism', but were happy to have links with such men as R. B. Jones, W. S. Jones and David Evans.

Evangelical ministers of churches and leaders of the new missionary societies were concerned with the decline in the theological colleges. There was a need not only to equip ministerial students but also Christian workers for every possible aspect of Christian work. The answer was found in the emerging Bible colleges. Here was an opportunity for believers, male and female, whatever their gifts, to be prepared for ministry. Fiedler comments on this development:[23]

The emphasis of faith missions of employing the neglected forces of Christianity created an institution which eventually strongly influenced not only faith missions, but also the whole of evangelical Christianity: that is, the Bible school . . . They were founded with a double edge: they were to provide the new (faith) missions, with trained missionaries, and they were to provide missionary training for those who had no chance of receiving any theological training in existing institutions, because they were not qualified and/or not wealthy enough to be accepted in them.

This, no doubt, was the outlook of R. B. Jones, and in 1916, leading up to the forming of his Bible School in 1919, he would be following an established tradition.

The first college of its kind in England was the East London Training Institute, opened in 1873 by Fanny and Grattan Guinness (of the family of brewing and banking fame), Grattan being a friend of Hudson Taylor. The aim was briefly and clearly defined, 'To multiply earnest and efficient missionaries at home and abroad'.[24] In fifteen years time, five

hundred workers had been trained there, seventy-
five of them joining the CIM. Grattan Guinness was
a key figure in this development, not only in England but in America and South Africa as well. Guinness directly influenced A. B. Simpson, who, in 1883,
set up the New York Bible Institute, closely allied
with the Christian Missionary Alliance, which he
had founded. When A. J. Gordon was considering
Bible work he discussed the matter with Guinness,
and this led to the formation of the Boston Bible Institute in 1889, which was closely linked with the
SIM (1900), and AIM (1895). A staunch supporter of
the launching of the AIM was A. T. Pierson, brought
up as a Presbyterian, who embraced the Holiness
Movement teaching, and who was present in Wales
during the Revival of 1904–05. The most influential
of all the institutes was the Moody Bible Institute
(1889), with R. A. Torrey, a person who was admired
by R. B. Jones, as the first director, although the foundation was laid by Emma Dryer, who sought the advice of Grattan Guinness. It is still a major influence
in evangelical circles: 'The Moody Bible Institute is
still, today, the major faith mission Bible school.'[25]

The East London Training Institute itself paved
the way for faith mission societies. One of its students, Samuel Bell, established the Qua Iboe Mission.
Karl Kumm, founder of SUM, which in the early
days had strong links with the ELTI, won C. T. Studd
over to mission work in Africa, which led to the
formation of WEC. When the ELTI closed in 1910, its
tradition was carried on by the Regions Beyond
Missionary Union, under the leadership of Gordon
Guinness, and F. B. Meyer as a director.

Parallel movements were taking place in other countries. In South Africa, Andrew Murray was the leading exponent of the Holiness Movement, and was in close touch with the Keswick leaders in England and Wales. In Scotland the Faith Mission came into being in 1886, with its own Bible College in Edinburgh, while the Bible Training Institute in Glasgow opened in 1892, patterned on the Moody Institute. Another development in England was the creation of the Pentecostal League in 1886 for the promotion of holiness, under whose auspices Oswald Chambers ran a Bible Training College in London from 1911 until 1915.

Most, if not all of these influences, were felt in Wales, with the Moody Institute gaining pride of place. Whenever R. B. Jones and W. S. Jones thought of the training of Christian workers they immediately referred to the Moody Institute. W. S. had visited the place during his stay in America, and it is significant, that, when some years later, D. M. Russell-Jones asked him for advice regarding going to a college, W. S. immediately urged him to go to Moody.[26] When the Joneses considered mission work overseas they would support the same faith missions as were supported by Moody, Boston, New York and Glasgow. R. B. Jones' thinking on these matters was moulded by the experiences of the Revival, holiness and advent teaching, the missionary enterprise of the faith missions and his own reading of Scripture. In 1916 he knew that it would be the day of small things, but the great day would dawn when the vision of a large Bible Institute would be established in Wales.[27]

The meeting of 31 August 1916 spurred R. B. Jones to challenge his people concerning overseas work. They were already contributing financially, but where were the missionaries? At the close of the service, 'The response was most cheering, for several rose to their feet signifying that if the Lord would so lead they were willing to go with Him to the ends of the earth'.[28] Those interested were formed into a class, and although no one went overseas immediately, some did go later. R. B. Jones' neighbour, Sidney Evans, was also interested in preparing men and women for Christian work, and the two joined forces, holding one meeting every week. Present at the first united meeting was a young lady who was committed to overseas work. Such an encouragement was taken as a sign of God's blessing, and the two men were joined by W. S. Jones to pray for future developments. The way was opened for the establishing of a Bible school. On 23 September 1919 the Bible Training School for Christian Workers came into being with eleven students, R. B. Jones being the tutor in charge, helped by W. W. Lewis, O. M. Owen, W. S. Jones. J. T. Phillips, J. R. Morgan, Keri Evans, who had been assistant to Edward Caird in Glasgow, and Sidney Evans, who, at the time, was thinking of going to India.[29] All of these men had been involved in the Revival, and were currently active in the witness of the *Efengylydd*, the Llandrindod Convention and the lesser conventions held in different parts of the country.

It was a small school, and the students paid £1.1s.0d. per term for their education. The curriculum was aimed at training workers for different aspects of Christian service, having an eye especially for those with very few educational opportunities. The efforts some of them made are portrayed by Brynmor Jones, like those who would attend class after a hard day's work in the coal-mine, or the wife that came in to take notes for her husband.[30] The main divisions of the course were: Study of the Bible, Missions, Christian Life and Service, Homiletics, Elements of Welsh and English, Greek Grammar (if required), and Practical Christian Work. As the Prospectus stated, 'The aim of the School is to provide mental, spiritual and practical training for young men and women of all denominations, who are desirous of entering upon any form of Christian work either at Home or Abroad'.[31]

Doctrinally, the main pillars of truth were: the infallibility of Scripture, the deity of Christ, the atoning sacrifice, the new birth and the second coming in terms of dispensational premillennialism. The leaders, especially R. B. Jones and W. S. Jones, were in complete agreement as to the ethos of the school, although there were differences in their respective emphases. R. B. was further removed than W. S. from denominational thinking, the latter being happy to take part in his denomination's activities. R. B. was ready to accept all kinds of believers, whatever their financial situation and irrespective of their educational ability. W. S. would have liked some of the students to go on to other colleges for a higher standard of education. Both the Joneses, however, were for expansion. R. B. Jones discussed the possibility with the Rev. J. R. Morgan (CM), Treharris, and Rees Howells (1875–1950), during 1922 and 1923.[32] Mr and

Mrs Howells had worked with the South Africa General Mission, and Mr Howells had known a crisis experience at one of the Llandrindod conventions.[33] Before leaving for Africa, Mrs Howells spent some time in the Faith College in Edinburgh, and the husband studied medicine at Livingstone College, London. In 1920 Rees Howells was commissioned by the Mission to work as a free lance with the main burden of reporting on the revival in Africa, and ministering in such a way that the people of God in Wales would cry for an awakening in their own land. R. B. Jones had his eye on Tynycymer Hall, Porth, but his hopes were not realized during months of discussion.

A divided army

Rees Howells believed that God was blessing to some extent, and those blessed needed to be taught. At the Llandrindod Convention of 1922 he made that need known, presenting the case that, 'they should ask the Lord for a training college'.[34] He had discussions with a number of ministers before leaving for America and while he was there was confirmed in his conviction that there was a need for an enlarged college in Wales, especially after visiting Moody Bible Institute. In his article in the *Efengylydd* he strongly argued for such an institution in Wales. Rees Howells did not feel that the necessary effort was being made in the country to meet with the needs of those who wanted to go overseas. He gave thanks for Porth and the great work the School had accomplished. Before it could be a success, it was essential to have a hostel for the students, basic costs to be low and tuition free.[35] The references to 'School' were vague. The term in one context would refer to the existing one in Porth, but Rees Howells also talked of a School for Wales, which could refer to Porth or a new institution.

On his return to Wales, discussions were renewed, but almost immediately R. B. Jones left for America, and he also was impressed by what he saw at the Moody Institute. While he was in America he still hoped that Rees Howells would support the Porth venture.[36] Slowly, however, by reading between the lines of letters from friends, he realized that Rees Howells was determined to act independently. R. B. believed, *'fy mod wedi dehongli'r sefyllfa yn bur agos'*, that is, that his interpretation was near the mark.[37] Although initially surprised, 'shocked and incredulous', at hearing what Rees Howells had in mind, R. B. Jones had come to clear conclusions before returning from America.[38]

While he was away the Principal of Porth had not received a word from Rees Howells. R. B. Jones expressed his feelings after returning:[39]

I am on my return confronted with an altogether changed plan, together with a fairly organised scheme for an institution on lines utterly distinct from those on which you and myself, from August 1922 to April 1923, worked so harmoniously.

Somewhere or other, since we last met, the enemy has crept in in his usual subtle way.

From June to September 1923 events happened quickly. At the Ammanford Convention, Rees Howells was convinced that the Lord was confirming to him

what was made known at Llandrindod in 1922, that
is, the need for a new college in Wales.[40] Immediately
after leaving Ammanford, Rees Howells conferred
with W. W. Lewis, Nantlais Williams and Keri Evans,
and encouraged by their support, believed that he
would be led to the right decision.[41] While on holiday
in Mumbles, near Swansea, he saw what was the
ideal place in Derwen Fawr Road. A ministers' meeting was convened,[42] and eventually in September he
went ahead to make arrangements to buy the building
in Derwen Fawr. Before that happened efforts were
made for Rees Howells and R. B. Jones to meet. Rees
Howells believed that what was needed was a ministers' meeting with both himself and R. B. Jones present, while the latter thought that the immediate need
was for the two of them to meet and discuss. There
was little hope for arranging any kind of meeting.[43]

The correspondence of the period is important,
not only to understand the tension between the leaders, but also to grasp the different outlook between
R. B. Jones and Rees Howells. The most revealing letter is the one written by R. B. Jones, in Welsh, to the
Rev. Nantlais Williams.[44] R. B. Jones expressed grief
in not being contacted concerning such an important
issue. He believed that his connection with Porth demanded some participation in the discussions. He
also had a lurking feeling that Rees Howells and
others were suggesting that Porth was a failure.[45] He
then proceeded to deal in more detail with some of
the central issues. The first point discussed was the
attitude to the denominational colleges. Rees Howells had argued that the new college would not com-
pete with the existing colleges. Said R. B., '*Rhwbiais fy*

llygaid, rhag fy mod yn methu darllen yn iawn', that is, 'I rubbed my eyes in case I was not reading correctly'[46] According to R. B. it was the very condition of these colleges that had led him in Wales, and others in other parts of Britain, to open Bible colleges.

Secondly, students of the new college would create a good relationship with denominational churches. The students would accept supplies on a regular basis, but according to R. B. this attitude was due to a lack of insight and vision. In order to win the favour of the churches, truth would have to be compromised, for if the students were uncompromising they would not be welcomed in the pulpits of Wales. Thirdly, there was the issue of academic standards. Rees Howells wanted a college that would be on the same standing as the best in the country, and John Thomas was a keen advocate of that view. 'The aim is to secure a band of ministers for Wales sound in doctrine and the equals of those turned out by the already recognized ministerial colleges in education and calibre',[47] or, as he said in another letter, the need was for 'consecrated scholarship'.[48] This was a real surprise for R. B. Jones, and referring specifically to Rees Howells, asked, 'What has come over our dear brother?'[49] Such talk was pandering to the flesh and losing sight of the wisdom of God which was made known in the foolishness of the cross. Education was essential, but consecration came before scholarship. The way forward, argued R. B. Jones, was by depending on the stone of David rather than trusting the sword of Goliath.

In closing R. B. Jones illustrated what he had in mind in terms of academic standards by referring to

particular persons, suggesting that W. S. Jones could
be compared favourably with Keri, and W. W. Lewis
with John Thomas. Lastly, R. B. referred to the col-
lecting which had taken place, and made the point
that at least part of the £500 should go to Porth Institute because it was that place that so many had in
mind when making their contributions. This was an
important aspect of the story as so much money was
involved, and many people felt that they had been
mis-led.

As far as the Swansea venture was concerned,
W. W. Lewis, John Thomas and Keri Evans were supportive.[50] John Thomas expressed his willingness to
travel the country on behalf of the new college and
was convinced that the contribution of both Porth
and Swansea was needed in Wales. Although supportive Keri Evans was uncertain regarding his particular role. When Rees Howells called to see him
during the middle of September 1923, he was anxious to know if there was a garden at the College,
and if there was one, then, perhaps, he could have a
job as a gardener.[51] This light-hearted reference is important as it reveals Keri Evans' thinking at the time.
It is obvious that he was not committed to teaching
in the new college. Men like W. S. Jones and Nantlais
Williams gave their support as they saw the need for
expansion, but their ideal would have been to have
one college in Wales with R. B. Jones taking a prominent part in its affairs. Nantlais, especially, was concerned with the unity of the brethren: not only was it
important for the present situation, but lack of unity
could hinder the blessing of God in revival. Nantlais,
and others, who were close to R. B., must have realized,

at least weeks before the opening of the college in
Swansea, that an united effort would not be possible.
Sincerely, and naïvely perhaps, Nantlais thought
that it was possible to support both ventures, while
others enlisted openly, and secretly, behind their
chosen captain.[52]

The College in Swansea opened in 1924 with Rees
Howells responsible for the arrangements, the Rev.
John Thomas, Myrtle Street, Liverpool, as Principal,
helped by Mr B. S. Fidler, Trelogan, Clwyd.[53] Mr Fidler
was in contact with the evangelicals of South Wales
through the Convention at Llandrindod and visits of
ministers to North Wales. It is possible that he was
present at one of the meetings to discuss the new college in Swansea, but it is known that his friend, the
Rev. J. Ellis Jones, Ffynnongroew, was present, and
they would have shared together the relevant issues.
J. Ellis Jones was present at the Ammanford Convention in 1922, when Rees Howells had spoken concerning mission, revival and the need for a training
college. During the period August to September
1923, Mr Fidler wondered if going to Swansea was
God's guidance for his life. He could see the need for
a new college, 'Its need is patent in view of the departure from the faith of the recognized colleges.'[54]
He would have liked to see Rees Howells and R. B.
Jones personally to discuss the situation with them,
but became convinced that it was right for him to go
to Swansea. On 9 June 1924, the opening day, B. S.
Fidler testified to God's grace in enabling him to respond to this new challenge. God had tested him like
the young man in Luke 18:22, but unlike the young
man, Fidler had been enabled to obey. It was a radical

change for him, as he was leaving a job for which he was being paid £360 per annum in order to live by faith, with a caravan as a home and a bicycle as a means of transport.[55]

B. S. Fidler was the son of William Fidler, a Baptist minister in Towcester, Northampton, where he laboured for over forty years.[56] The son was drawn to Wales by the Revival of 1904-05 and was so anxious to be near the sphere of its influence that he moved, first to Gronant and then to Trelogan, North Wales. He was preaching in the district during 1905.[57] The area was not only blessed during 1904, but also during the earlier visits of Richard Owen, and many of the villagers remembered those times of refreshing.[58] Mr Fidler became the headmaster of the village school at Trelogan in 1908, and his skill and efficiency won the commendation of the school inspectors.[59] He had the privilege of teaching David Lloyd, the renowned tenor, and Emlyn Williams, the eminent author.[60] The school, and the headmaster, featured in the film, 'The Corn is Green'. At Trelogan Fidler revealed his flair for languages and soon mastered the Welsh language. He also revealed his enthusiasm for evangelism and biblical teaching. At Oxton, the small Baptist chapel in the village, he had a Bible class, following in 1923, 'The Whole Bible Sunday School Lesson Course'. He prepared thoroughly and had a plan of study to give to every member of the class.[61]

Though happy in teaching his class, Fidler wanted to extend his sphere of influence in order to help Christians in the area, not just in Trelogan. He, with the Rev. J. Ellis Jones, saw the need for helping believers, and organized conventions, resembling those in Ammanford, Porth and other places in Wales. David Evans, Bridgend, visited in 1923, and the speakers for 1924 were J. Macdonald, India, and J. Ellis Jones himself.[62] This was a work which was near to their heart, and Mr Fidler must have missed his friend when he moved to South Wales. The schoolmaster was highly respected in the area and a good congregation was present at Oxton, 24 September 1924, to wish him well in his new work, when J. Ellis Jones and John Thomas, Liverpool, were the preachers. The Spirit of God moved in the meeting, and at the close of the service the congregation responded willingly to a call of consecration.[63]

As the three men in the new college settled down there were great expectations for the coming first year and all went well until the summer of 1925, when their dreams were shattered. Rees Howells claimed that the Lord had revealed to him that a storm was brewing and when it raged in September and October, it created havoc in the College. There were tensions between Rees Howells and the students and between him and the staff. In his account of the story, Norman Grubb refused to go into details, but in what he said came down clearly on Rees Howell's side: 'There was worldliness among the students and unwillingness for the standards of faith and surrender which the Holy Spirit had said were to be presented and maintained in the College'.[64]

Not all of those involved with the College would agree with that assessment; indeed, the majority would disagree. Norman Grubb concentrates on the students, but what was their response? The vast majority of the thirty-eight students were very unhappy, although Rees Howells believed that he had strong grounds for applying discipline when he found out that some of the students were smoking.[65] The students, however, described the demands made upon them in the College as 'tyranny' and the charges brought against one of them as 'flimsy' and 'absurd'.[66] They had received an Eisteddfod Programme with an invitation to take part in the competitions. The student representative, T. J. Phillips, asked for John Thomas' opinion, who expressed the view that there was nothing wrong in accepting the invitation. Rees Howells reacted strongly, accusing the students of being worldly and he expelled Phillips.[67] John Thomas made it quite clear that he was on the side of the students and made that known to the whole student body, but felt that it was his duty to remain for a while in spite of the difficult situation.[68]

B. S. Fidler was even more unsettled and eventually found it impossible to stay. A statement by the students gives a glimpse into the change that had taken place: 'The whole atmosphere of the college had changed completely, and the students wrapped in an atmosphere of continual friction and unhappiness'.[69] Matters came to a head in early October:[70]

The college has collapsed. All the students leave today. A policy of harshness and tyrrany (sic) has alienated them all! These were the words of one of the most enthusiastic supporters of the new venture, and the one made principal. No wonder he exclaimed, 'What a lesson and warning!'

Students left and there were no lectures for a whole year. Fidler felt that the confusion was intolerable, and he resigned. Peace was restored, new students accepted and the College developed, but on very different lines from those discussed during 1922 to 1924. The one remaining characteristic was the principle of living by faith. The academic standards mentioned were not pursued and a very hard line was taken as far as denominations were concerned.

Continuing warfare

Almost immediately B. S. Fidler, and some of the students, moved to Porth to join R. B. Jones. Mr Fidler agreed to go before the end of 1925 and started on his work in January 1926. This was a timely provision for the Institute at Porth because one of the visiting lecturers, Seth Joshua, had just died in 1925, another lecturer, Keri Evans, had been ill during 1924, and T. M. Jeffreys,[71] who had taken his place, only stayed for a few months. After spending some time with Austin Sparks at the Baptist Church, Honor Oak, London, Jeffreys was appointed co-pastor before the end of 1925.[72] R. B. Jones refers to the step of faith in calling Mr Fidler:[73]

Last year, Mr B. S. Fidler was appointed resident Tutor. This was a new and responsible venture. Up till then, owing to the fact that all the other Tutors held pastorates, the tuition cost the School nothing; it was all a labour of love. Mr Fidler, having no other means of livelihood, had to be assigned a certain remuneration. This meant an addition of £208 per annum, in a word, the doubling of our expenditure.

Mr Fidler settled down quickly, being responsible for teaching General Knowledge, English, Practical Evangelism, in which he was helped by others, and New Testament Greek.

Apart from the Institute, Fidler found other channels of service. He was responsible for the children's corner in the *Efengylydd*,[74] and was always ready to contend for the faith, although he could not be termed an 'astute apologist'.[75] On one occasion he was taken to task by *Yr Hauwr* for his exposition of the faith.[76] There was an opportunity also to work in, and from the Tabernacle. Fidler was made an associate minister with special responsibility for developing the work at Mount Pleasant, an offshoot of Tabernacle. Many of the Porth students were active with this work, including Bronwen Hale, who was to marry A. L. Hughes, India, and Grangetown, Cardiff. The two sisters employed by Tabernacle also helped, and one of them, Miss Ellis, became more than a co-worker as she and B. S. Fidler became husband and wife.[77]

The Principal, R. B. Jones, died in 1933, followed in a few months by W. S. Jones. The loss of such a character as R. B. Jones was soon felt in the Institute and amongst its supporters. He had held them together and had ruled the Institute with an iron hand. The vacuum left behind gave room for tensions, made worse by a lack of finance. Some supporters believed that D. M. Phillips was pushing himself forward to be Principal, while others thought that Geraint, R. B.'s son, was the right person for the post. B. S. Fidler was chairman of the Board, but was very unhappy with the situation. Numerous attempts were made to call the Directors together, but to no avail, most of them making excuses for not attending.[78] Probably they were unwilling to face up to the real reasons, those being financial, doctrinal and personal difficulties. Those real reasons emerged clearly during 1935. As a result of the slump in America very little money was coming in from that country. This made a marked difference to the finances, as the miners in Pennsylvania especially had been faithful supporters of the Institute. D. M. Phillips continued to assert his authority, and matters came to a head, personally, when B. S. Fidler proposed that one of the men from Toronto should be appointed as the Principal of the Institute. This move was blocked by D. M. Phillips who chaired the meeting. The end result was that Phillips himself was appointed. He immediately started to economize by dismissing the gardener, and took over some of Mr Fidler's lectures, which, the Principal believed, was another way of cutting costs, but Fidler himself felt that he was not wanted.[79]

Fidler, F. S. Copleston, and others, also doubted the theological orthodoxy of one of their colleagues, especially when that person gave a lecture on 'The Ignorance of Christ'.[80] Implied in the lecture was an acceptance of the 'Kenosis' theory concerning the incarnation of the Lord Jesus Christ.[81] As far as the two mentioned were concerned this was just a subtle way of introducing modernism. At first a little would be yielded and that would lead to more and more being taken away from the faith once and for all delivered to the saints.

The Porth lecturers were also wary because the colleague who had given the lecture was a product of the University College of Wales, Cardiff, where modernism had made real headway. The lecturer concerned had been introduced to Kirsopp Lake's

The Beginning of Christianity, and was much impressed with it. Lake provided the lecturer with a
framework to look at the New Testament, which was
very different from that adopted at Porth. Accepting
the presuppositions of Harnack, Lake argued for the
late date of Acts, its composite sources and interpol-
ations in Paul's Epistles.[82] Such an approach to the
New Testament fitted in neatly with the change of attitude to the Person of the Lord Jesus Christ. It is true
that the moderate kenotics acknowledged that Jesus
Christ was the Son of God, but in coming to earth of
what did he empty himself? (Phil. 2:7). If the Son became truly human it must be that he had willingly
accepted some limitations, and attempts were made
to identify them. There were variations within this
school of thought, but the main approach was to distinguish between the 'natural' and 'moral' attributes
of God, or the 'relative' and 'immanent' attributes.
Examples of the relative would be omniscience and
omnipresence, while examples of the immanent
would be love and holiness. According to the kenotic
teaching the Son of God laid aside the former but re-
tained the latter.

There is no doubt that this teaching detracted
from the Person of the God-man, and it was good
and proper that Fidler and others reacted strongly
against it. On the other hand it is a pity that those
who held the view were attacked as modernists,
while many of them, including Delitzsch and T. C.
Edwards, were making a genuine attempt to grasp
the mystery of the incarnation. Others did develop
the doctrine in such a way that only the man Christ
Jesus was left.[83] Personal tensions, however, were not

conducive to healthy theological discussions.

Fidler, as chairman of the Board was conscious of a lack of support and considered not going to an important meeting in February 1936. He was also grieved that money promised to him was not forthcoming. He felt now that the end was in sight. He informed J. R. Morgan, the secretary, in February 1936, 'Another student has left—Kirslake from Barry. The Mission supporting him have withdrawn him'.[84] The teacher had been led to lecture at Swansea and led on to Porth. Once again B. S. Fidler felt that it was time for him to move. The destination was Barry, a place not unknown to him, as God had already introduced him to that town.

REFERENCES

1. 'Inception', *Prospectus of The South Wales Bible Training Institute, Porth*, 1931, 'the purpose of the visit was to interest the Church in missionary work generally and to solicit prayer for her own special work'. The lady was Miss Evans from Port Talbot, 'The Bible Training School for Christian Workers', *Yr Efengylydd*, Nov.–Dec., 1919.

2. Cynog Williams, 'Milwr Da i Iesu Grist', *Yr Efengylydd*, May 1933. The Club had a Roman Catholic connotation.

3. Background: Brynmor Pierce Jones, 'A Biographical Study of R. B. Jones', unpublished work, 55-71; Eifion Evans, *The Welsh Revival of 1904* (Evangelical Press of Wales, 1969), chapters 4 and 5.

4. W. S. Jones: *Yr Efengylydd*, Oct.–Nov., 1933; *Seren Gomer*, May 1935; Keri Evans, *My Spiritual Pilgrimage* (James Clark, 1961), Section VII, where he also refers to the influence of Henry Drummond.

5. Keri Evans, op. cit.

6. Brynmor Pierce Jones, *The King's Champions* (The Author, Glascoed, Gwent, 1986 ed.), 97, and 98 for the pioneers of the venture. Originally it was the *Mill Street Magazine*, letter T. R. Williams, 22 June 1965, R. B. Jones Papers, No. 35. (NLW).

7. Aberystwyth, NLW, CMA, 28, 228. For the main Llandrindod Convention, Brynmor Pierce Jones, *The Spiritual History of the Keswick in*

Wales (B. P. Jones, Christian Literature Press, 1989), and for Amman-ford, J. D. Williams, *Cynhadledd Sulgwyn Rhydaman* (Rhydaman, d.d).

8. R. B. Jones, *Rent Heavens* (Porth, Foreword 1930), 87-88; reports appeared regularly in the *Efengylydd*.

9. *A Witness and a Minister*, 1925, 4.

10. The best summary is in Welsh, Gwilym H. Jones, 'Beirniadaeth yr Hen Destament yng Nghymru, 1890–1914', *Y Gair a'r Genedl* (Abertawe, 1982), gol. E. Stanley John.

11. *Ffydd ac Argyfwng Cenedl*, Cyfrol 2 (Abertawe, 1982), 104.

12. Dewi Eirug Davies, *Hoff Ddysgedig Nyth* (Abertawe, 1976), 195.

13. Pennar Davies, gol. *Athrawon ac Annibynwyr* (Abertawe, 1971), 92.

14. Alan P. F. Sell, *Theology in Turmoil* (Baker Book, 1986), 33.

15. All the Welsh names, but for Thomas Lewis, are found in the *Dictionary of Welsh Biography Down to 1940* (1959), and vol. 2, 1941–50 (1970); for Thomas Lewis, *Athrawon ac Annibynwyr*, op. cit.

16. *Rent Heavens*, op. cit., 90; 'It is a most remarkable fact that, almost without exception, all who entered definitely and fully into Revival blessing became pre-millennialist in their view of the Advent'; ibid., 91.

17. Ibid, 91.

18. Klaus Fiedler, *The Story of Faith Missions* (Regnum Lynx, 1994), 144; Brynmor Pierce Jones, unpublished work, op. cit., 165, 278.

19. Fiedler, op. cit., 277.

20. Ibid.

21. Ian M. Randall, 'Spiritual Renewal and Social Reform', *The Evangelical Quarterly*, 1983, especially 72-5.

22. Ibid, 80. 'Except on a firm and well-defined "fundamentalist" basis, I, like yourselves have no interest in this or any other work', R. B. Jones to two sisters, 31 July 1926, Aberystwyth, R. B. Jones Papers. R. B. Jones and J. R. Morgan were aware, however, of developments in the University Colleges, and influenced some of the early leaders of the IVF, Geraint D. Fielder, *'Excuse me, Mr Davies—Hallelujah!'* (Inter-Varsity Press and Evangelical Press of Wales, 1983), 37, 41-2, 53, 56; other links, 81. Also, prominent reformed theologians visited Porth, including Gresham Machen, Geoffrey Thomas, 'J. Gresham Machen in the United Kingdom', *Banner of Truth*, July 1983; Visitors' Book, R. B. Jones' Papers.

23. Klaus Fiedler, op. cit., 144.

24. Ibid, 145, and for the history of the Guinness family, Michele Guinness, *The Guinness Legend* (Hodder and Stoughton, 1989), a thrilling story, although disappointing on the College aspect, note, 100, 118-19, 231-2, 286-87.

25. Fiedler, op. cit., 147.

26. D. M. Russell-Jones Papers, Bryntirion, Bridgend.

27. 'The Bible Training School for Christian Workers', *Yr Efengylydd*, Nov.–Dec., 1919; *A Witness and a Minister*, 1925.

28. *Yr Efengylydd*, 1919, op. cit.,

29. Brynmor Pierce Jones, *The King's Champions*, op. cit., has 3 September 1919 and 8 students; *Witness and a Ministers*, 1925, has 23 September and 10 students—this was a reprint of an article published in 1919, 'The Bible Training School for Christian Workers', op. cit., which is reproduced word for word in the Institute *Prospectus* for 1931, except for the number of students, which is given as 11. In agreement with the *Prospectus: Rent Heavens*, op. cit., 88, and 'Dros Dir a Môr', *Yr Efengylydd*, February 1929. Sidney Evans left for India in 1920.

30. *The King's Champions* op. cit., 235-6; idem, unpublished work, 335f.

31. Report of opening, *Yr Efengylydd*, Nov–Dec., 1919.

32. R. B. Jones Papers, No. 18, Letter, 7 September 1923, Rees Howells to R. B. Jones. According to F. S. Copleston, Rees Howells had promised to help Porth, financially, Kevin Adams Papers, Bryntirion, Bridgend.

33. For Rees Howells, Norman Grubb, *Rees Howells, Intercessor* (Lutterworth, 1952, 1969); Doris M. Ruscoe, *The Intercession of Rees Howells* (Guildford-Ft Washington, 1983).

34. *Yr Efengylydd*, September 1922.

35. 'Ysgol Feiblaidd i Gymru', *Yr Efengylydd*, June 1923. While in America, Rees Howells visited Moody, Philadelphia and Toronto Bible Institutes.

36. 'Taith y Parch. R. B. Jones yn America', *Yr Efengylydd*, 1923, letter dated 16 July 1923.

37. R. B. Jones' Papers, letter 14 September 1923, R. B. Jones to Nantlais.

38. R. B. Jones had a clearer understanding of the situation than that suggested by Brynmor Pierce Jones, unpublished work, op. cit., 333 n. 25. According to Mrs Menna Bowen, R. B. Jones' daughter, it was Graham Scroggie who gave the information to her father; interview Mrs Bowen, 28 October 1995.

39. R. B. Jones' Papers, letter 6 October 1923, R. B. Jones to Rees Howells; earlier, R. B. Jones had written, 'The Lord has so very definitely laid the work of the Bible School here in my hands and, without his consent I could not relinquish that in order to join in a project which to me does not seem to have quite the same purpose nor to proceed on quite the same lines', 14 September 1923.

40. Norman Grubb, op. cit., 184-5. On the basis of 1 Chronicle 28:20-1, 29:4, he was encouraged to go on, and also pray for the 'talent' men-

tioned in 29:4, which, from the margin of his Scofield Bible, he learned was worth £6,150.

41. Rees Howells had made known his views at the Ammanford Convention (Whitsun), but Keri Evans was not present, and, therefore he invited the Carmarthen minister, Nantlais Williams and W. W. Lewis to a meeting at Mumbles, R. B. Jones' Papers, 7 September 1923.

42. Ibid. The meeting was attended by the Revs Wynne Evans, W. S. Jones, W. W. Lewis, Nantlais Williams, Phillips (Pem.), John Ellis Jones and others. They agreed to proceed with the purchase. At least one other meeting was held, Keri Evans to R. B. Jones, 24 September 1923. Brynmor Pierce Jones, says that the trustees were 'certain friends' of Rees Howells 'such as T. M. Lloyd, David Evans and W. W. Lewis', *The King's Champions,* op. cit., 221. Norman Grubb says that the trustees were W. W. Lewis, Henry Griffiths and Rees Howells, *Rees Howells,* op. cit., 196; also 'God's College', *South Wales Daily Post,* 10 June 1924.

43. R. B. Jones' Papers, attempts to meet, Letters, 4, 6, 8, 9, 12, 13, 15, 17, 18, 24, October 1923, but the correspondence continued until 12 November.

44. Ibid, 14 September 1923.

45. R. B. Jones demanded an answer from Rees Howells regarding the relationship of the two colleges. Was the new college a 'development', a 'supplement' or a 'substitute'?, 13, 18 October 1923; Rees Howells replied that in the light of R. B. Jones' response it had to be a supplement, 30 October 1923, contrary to what Brynmor Pierce Jones says, *The King's Champions,* op. cit., 223.

46. Ibid, 14 September 1923.

47. Ibid, letter of John Thomas, 21 August 1923.

48. Ibid, 27 September, October 1923.

49. Ibid, 14 September 1923.

50. John Thomas, letters, op. cit., R. B. Jones Papers; Norman Grubb, op. cit., 187, 196.

51. Ibid., Keri Evans to R. B. Jones, 24 September 1923.

52. Even those who supported Rees Howells could be critical of him, e.g., Nantlais to R. B. Jones, 17 September, W. S. Jones to R. B. Jones, 17 October, 1923.

53. Opening: 'Cyrddau Agoriadol', *Yr Efengylydd,* 1924; 'God's College', *South Wales Evening Post,* op. cit.

54. R. B. Jones' Papers, W. S. Jones to R. B. Jones, 16 October 1923. For J. Ellis Jones, CMA, 21, 415.

55. *Yr Efengylydd,* 1924, op. cit.

56. The middle name is 'Sheppard', as he was descended from the old

Puritan family. When William Fidler went to Towcester there was division. He formed a new church and in 1877 a new chapel was built, 'He returned to his old trade and made furniture in order to raise money, working so steadily and successfully, in this and other ways, that his twenty-sixth anniversary as minister, in 1897, was celebrated by the clearing off of the whole debt on the new premises and the presentation to Mr Fidler of £50 as a mark of esteem and affection', E. A. Payne, *The Baptists of Towcester* (Northampton, 1936), 17.

57. Letters from his parents to Bernard S. Fidler (1905–12), presented to the author by the Rev. Ken Peel, Yeovil.

58. Account of the area, with references to Mr Fidler, *Deugain Mlynedd yn Nhrelogan, 1910–1950* (Yr Wyddgrug, n.d.), 8.

59. Mr Fidler started on his duties on 1 September 1908, when 91 scholars were admitted to the School. David Lloyd's home was next door to the School. 'Oct. 3rd 1924. The duties of Mr B. S. Fidler the headmaster terminated this day'; information kindly sent by Mr Alwyn Roberts, the present headmaster of the School.

60. School Register, Trelogan.

61 'Dros Dir a Môr', *Yr Efengylydd*, December 1923,

62. Ibid, April 1924.

63. 'Trelogan a Newmarket', *Y Goleuad*, 1 November 1924 (7); *Deugain Mlynedd*, op. cit.

64. Norman Grubb, op. cit., 198.

65. F. S. Copleston from Kevin Adams Papers.

66. Statement by Students, 7 October 1925, R. B. Jones' Papers.

67. Copleston from Kevin Adams Papers; interview Noel Gibbard, 16 June 1995.

68. R. B. Jones' Papers, op. cit.

69. Statement of Students, op. cit. F. S. Copleston went there as a student in October 1924 and he confirms this reference. Copleston left Manchester Baptist College because of the liberalism taught there, moved to Swansea, considered joining the Rev. D. T. Morgan, who had formed a Missionary Society on evangelical principles, but he died, and Copleston went on to Porth with R. B. Jones; interview Copleston 16 June 1995, op. cit.

70. R. B. Jones' Papers, letter 7 October 1925, signature torn off, but added in pencil, 'Rev. John Thomas'.

71. Jeffreys, when at Ebbw Vale, had been influenced by reports of Revival meetings under Alexander Boddy in Sunderland. A 'wonderful praise meeting' was held in Jeffreys's study, and Waunllwyd, Ebbw Vale, became a centre of blessing, Colin Whittaker, *Seven Pentecostal Leaders* (Marshalls, 1983), 49.

72. Ibid.

73 R. B. Jones' Papers, 31 July 1926, R. B. Jones to Cory sisters.

74. He wrote regularly to this section for over ten years.

75. Brynmor Pierce Jones, unpublished work, op. cit., 233.

76. *The King's Champions*, op. cit. 144, where he gives *Yr Hauwr* as the source, but unpublished work, op. cit., 214 gives *Seren Cymru*, 28 January 1927, as the source.

77. Miss Ellis had personal supervision of the female students and lived in the Institute, *A Witness and a Minister*, December 1927; Church Manual, 1940, *The Tabernacle, Porth*, Jubilee Souvenir, 1874–1924.

78. The Directors were: Rev. B. S. Fidler, Chairman of Board, Mr T. H. Morgan, Hon. Tr., Rev. J. R. Morgan, Sec., Rev. G. Ll. Jones, Miss A. Edmunds, Rev. W. Nantlais Williams, Rev. David Evans, Rev. George Douglas and Mr Pryce Lewis, *A Witness and a Minister*, October 1934. Correspondence to call meetings, R. B. Jones' Papers, from 15 February 1936.

79. 'So Dr Phillips has jumped into office before the matter is settled by the Directors and furthermore rushed to print. Who are the Directors now? I believe the co-opted ones are out after 12 months unless re-elected. Is this so?' Fidler to J. R. Morgan, 15 Feb. 1936, R. B. Jones' Papers, No. 18.

80. Copleston: Kevin Adams and Noel Gibbard, op. cit. A former student, Gordon Diamond, could say of 1931, 'I remember heavy stress on the Kenotic problem', Brynmor Pierce Jones Papers, Bryntirion.

81. H. R. Mackintosh, *The Doctrine of the Person of Christ* (T. and T. Clark, 1st ed. 1912, reprint 1923); D. M. Baillie, *God Was in Christ* (London, 1948; 1977 ed.), 94ff.

82. Kirsopp Lake (1872–1946), works include, *The Earlier Epistle of Paul* (1913), with Foakes Jackson, *The Beginnings of Christianity* (1920–3), and 'His book *Historical Evidence for the Resurrection* (1907) was an attempt to cast doubt on the story of the empty tomb', J. D. Douglas, ed., *New International Dictionary of the Christian Church* (Paternoster, 1974).

83. Berkouwer points out that the view leads, as with Gess, to the man Christ Jesus, 'Thus we observe that this Christology, when consistent, arrives at a view which leaves room for nothing but the man Jesus Christ', *The Person of Christ* (Eerdmans, 1984 ed.), 29.

84. Fidler to J. R. Morgan, op. cit.

2.
Battling at Barry
1936–1939

In 1880 Barry was a small village, but by the end of the century had grown considerably. The first passenger train from Barry to Cardiff ran in 1883 and the first ship entered Barry Docks in 1889.[1] Work was available, not only for the locals, but for many from outside as well, making Barry a cosmopolitan town. Some worked for a particular period while others settled down and made the place their new home. The growth gave the churches and the evangelistic agencies a new opportunity to take the gospel to many more people. It is significant that in 1939, many churches, as well as the town, were celebrating their jubilee. Among them was Court Road Methodist Church, a cause rooted in the work of the Bible Christian Church in Cardiff, whose members grasped the opportunity to evangelize in Barry. Another aspect of the missionary approach was the coming of the Welsh Congregationalists from Penarth to promote the Welsh language witness to the gospel.[2]

Geographically, Barry was situated in a remote part of the country, and even during the early period of growth an advert appeared in a particular paper, in reply to an enquiry from Barry, 'We shall be pleased to quote if you would kindly let us know where Barry is.'[3] Soon, there was no need to enquire as the name of the town became known world-wide because of its export of coal and students and import of bananas from many countries. Progress was stemmed by the strikes of 1921 and 1926, and ten years later the cloud of unemployment was still hanging over the town. Those outside and inside the churches had to make efforts to meet, as effectively as possible, their particular needs.

Many churches endeavoured to face the period of hardship by renewing efforts with their cultural and social activities. Members had to be kept together and encouraged, and, at the same time, many of the activities arranged would bring in a little money for the upkeep of the building. A local correspondent quoted from an address given in one of the chapels, when the speaker had said that, 'The churches today experience great difficulty in meeting overhead charges owing to the present depression and were therefore, resorting to various means of raising the money'.[4] It would have been possible, in 1936, to attend a musical evening, a cantata, oratorio, a lecture or a garden party, which would meet with some of the needs of the members and help to fill the rather empty coffers of the churches.

One church decided to invite a controversial minister to be the guest preacher, and the Rev. Tom Nefyn Williams came to the annual meeting.[5] He was a converted man, who had spent a few months with R. B. Jones in Porth, but developed as an unorthodox teacher, was dismissed from the Welsh Presbyterian Church of Wales, but welcomed back a few years later. A different approach was adopted by

the Melrose Mission Hall (Plymouth Brethren). Being
commited to the gospel of salvation by grace alone,
they held a fortnight's crusade, to the astonishment
of one local reader, who marvelled at the fact that the
Mission could venture in such a way at such a time.
Another church invited Dr Martyn Lloyd-Jones,
Sandfields, Aberavon, to be the guest preacher. He
was a Calvinistic Methodist in the true sense of the
word, holding strongly to the Calvinism of the
Methodist fathers and to their evangelistic zeal. In
that particular sermon he demonstrated clearly that
the main opposition to the simple, old-fashioned
gospel, was not intellectual, but material.[6] Evidences
of that tradition were found in the Forward Movement Halls in Barry Island and Barry Dock. The latter was opened in 1903, one year prior to the Revival,
and is also of interest as it brings together industrial
development and church growth, not only in general
terms, but also as regards one particular person.
Lord Davies, Llandinam, the man responsible for
opening up the docks, gave his support and name to
Dinam Hall, Barry Docks.

Another strand in the evangelical tradition was
the evangelical missions and conventions organized
across denominational boundaries. It would have
been possible to visit a convention in Barry in 1936,
of the same kind as those held in Porth and Ammanford, reflecting the main convention in Llandrindod.
Indeed, the event in Barry was called the Barry
Keswick Convention.[7] The officials included the Rev.
J. W. Owen, Cardiff, chairman, who will be prominent in future chapters of this story, the Rev. and Mrs
Ackland, Barry, and Miss B. M. Stephens, Tyla Morris,

Pentyrch. The Acklands and Miss Stephens were an integral part of the growth of mission work in Barry, a work represented by Luchana Mission Hall in the town.

The beginnings of such a work can be traced to the Christian Excavators Union of 1875. Mrs Garnet, the founder, worked in close association with three South Wales ladies, Miss B. M. Allen, Miss Picton and Mrs F. de Courcy Hamilton.[8] The mission in Barry was located in different places until 1929 when Luchana was built as a memorial to Mrs Courcy Hamilton. Mr and Mrs Hamilton had done much missionary work overseas, especially in Spain, including Luchana in that country, and this explains the name given to the mission in Barry. To confirm the work Mr Hamilton opened a mission, named Montserrat, in Hirwaun Street, another reminder of overseas work, and Wilberforce Hall, a reminder of the emancipation of the slaves.

De Courcy Hamilton was a director of the Coal Exchange in Cardiff,[9] had been a staunch supporter of the Porth Bible Institute, had contributed financially to its upkeep and had advised on structural changes to the building.[10] Miss B. M. Stephens was on his staff and became his secretary. Knowing B. S. Fidler personally, Mr Hamilton invited him, in 1935, to take charge of the Luchana Mission. The Institute lecturer was glad of the opportunity to concentrate on evangelism, a work so close to his heart. He had a deep desire to reach the men on the railway and in the docks. He wanted to see the work of the Mission continuing effectively, and fulfil faithfully the aim of the founders. Then apart from the men on the railway and in the docks there were the thousands who flocked to the sands to enjoy themselves, about 80,000 during the summer period. Fidler committed himself to the work, and would bring down the students from Porth to help him with the open-air services on the sands in Barry Island.[11]

In twelve months time Mr Hamilton was the means of extending the boundaries of Mr Fidler's sphere of influence, although it only meant occupying one building next door to the Mission, but in terms of future influence it made the world a parish for Mr Fidler. As the sovereign God could link Colossae and Rome, God was preparing to link Barry with the four corners of the world. Standing near Luchana was a large, vacant building, intended as a hotel, but proved a white elephant.[12] One suggestion is that the interested party could not get a licence to sell alcohol. That failure led to the opening of the place for those licensed from heaven to preach the good news of salvation in the Lord Jesus Christ. Mr Hamilton bought the building, and, initially, thought of turning it into flats, but conscious of the situation in Porth, offered the place to Mr Fidler as a Bible school to train Christian workers.

He accepted the offer gladly, and prepared immediately to occupy the place for such work, while he and Mrs Fidler continued to live at Luchana. He was a man that could give himself to the study of languages and enjoy preaching in open-air services, but he could also put on his apron and do some decorating. Much of the internal preparation was done by Mr Fidler himself, with a few willing hands to help. Some of the books and some of the furniture were brought from Tynycymer Hall, Porth, which, on the one hand, must have grieved Mr Fidler, as it reminded him of the tension of 1934–36, while, on the other hand, it gladdened his heart, because a new beginning was now possible.

Students and staff

Such was the enthusiasm that it was decided to commence the work in May 1936. With such short notice it was surprising that there was a response in terms of students, but a few came, seven in May, according to the Log Book, eight in October and two in November. The Register, however, gives eight for May, the reason being that there was one day-student. The Barry School of Evangelism opened on 5 May 1936:[13]

Barry students, May 1936. *From left to right, back row:* Vernon Parfitt, George Cole, Leslie Stevenson, George McClelland. *Front row:* Ernest Ridout, Clifford Evans, Alwyn Rees, Mrs Fidler, Mr B. S. Fidler

The School opened with seven students—Mr L. G. Cole, Mr L. Stevenson, Mr T. C. Evans, Mr A. Rees, Mr G. McClelland, Mr E. Ridout and Mr V. Parfitt.

The opening devotional meeting was presided over by F. de Courcy Hamilton, Esq., Rev. J. W. Owen (Cardiff), Capt. Alister Smith and Rev. F. S. Copleston among others were present.

The Register of Admissions gives more detail:[14]

HOME ADDRESS

McClelland, Gerald W.	113 Castlereagh Road, Belfast	1936–37 Christian Colporteurs, S.A.S.R.A.
Ridout, Ernest J.	90 Ystrad y Waun, Pencoed Bridgend, Glam.	1936–37 Pastor Presb. Chr.
Parfitt, Vernon	64 Ynys Terrace, Rhydfelin Pontypridd	1936–38 School Teaching
Evans, Clifford T.	8 Bigyn Park Terrace Llanelly	1936–37 Brazil invalided home,Builth Wells, secular work
Stephens, J. Leslie	30 Islington Road, Southville	May 1936–Dec. 1936
Rees, Alwyn	Wernlas, 20 Elizabeth Street Llanelly	1936–37 Angola Mission
Cole, L. George	35 Johnston Street, Cricklewood	1936 Secretary & Treasurer of the Barry School of Evangelism, lay pastor Gloucester
Wagstaff, Grace	98 Queen Street, Barry, Glam.	1936–38 [day student]

Eight were accepted in September:[15]

Minton, Clarice A.	65 Clydach Street, Brynmawr, Brecs.	1936–37 Billingsgate Medical Mission Colportage
McHaffie, James	. 125 Castlereagh Rd., Belfast	Barry School of Evangelism, Hengoed, Cardiff Dock Baptist Ch., West Drayton Baptist Church
Jackson, Stanley	Varley Field, Bracewell	1936–38 Ackhill; Essex
Philips, Elizabeth Gwyneth (Mrs Thomas)	9 Marble Hall, Llanelly	1936–38 Nurse, Cardiff City Lodge, Mrs Thomas 'The Croft', Llandeilo

Price, Frank Oswald	Broad Oak, Abbey Cwm Hir, Penybont, Rads.	1936–38 farmer, preacher, 'Vron Cottage', Abbey Cwm Hir
Chapman, Wilfred	44 Holford Avenue, Bescob Grange, Walsall	1936–38 Bulwell, Notts. Oldham, Lancs., Pwllgwaun, Langley, Slough
Carpenter, Gwladys	35 Ashton Lane, Perry Bar Birmingham	1936–38 Now Mrs Arthur
Phipps, Edward	6 Newbridge Road Pontllanfraith, Mon.	1936–37 secular employment, preacher, surface worker

Two in October:

Gordon, William James	78 Hatton Drive, Woodstock Rd., Belfast	1936–38
Kitchen, Nathanael	29 Ribble St., Belfast	1936–38 Deacon-Presbyterian Church. Attending Grove Baptist Chapel. Engaged in Male Voice Praise Work

The links with Porth were very strong. Ernest Ridout, a Porth student, moved to Barry in May, followed by Ted Phipps in September. Mr Courcy Hamilton had a long-established relationship with the Institute, and a zealous supporter of the new venture was the Rev. J. R. Morgan, Treharris, Mid Glam., secretary and lecturer at the Institute, assistant to R. B. Jones, and who was, later, to lecture at the new school. The same was true of the Rev. Copleston, who was also an assistant to R. B. Jones, and was present at the opening on 5 May. T. Knight Jenkins, Penarth and Cardiff, was a trustee of the Institute and faithfully served on the Barry Council for many years as treasurer.

Most of the staff were Porth men. Mr Fidler himself was in charge, supported by his dear wife. He

gave up his work at Luchana in 1937, in order to concentrate on the School, but he was also unhappy
with the set form of worship that he was expected to
conduct, Mr Hamilton being a keen Anglican. Added to these two aspects was the fact that Mr Fidler
accepted believers' baptism only. Apart from caring
for the material needs of the students, Mrs Fidler
was responsible for the Singing Lessons and was regarded as a member of staff. A visiting lecturer was
Alister Smith of the Salvation Army, tall, erect and
forthright, who had rendered the same service to the
Institute at Porth. Two of the lecturers were former
Porth students, Ivor Powell and Glyndwr Davies.

School group, May 1936. *From left to right, front row:* F. de Courcy
Hamilton, J. W. Owen, Mrs Fidler, B. S. Fidler, Alister Smith,
Miss B. M. Stephens, F. S. Copleston

One of the 1936 students refers to Ivor Powell's
popularity. 'He was as popular with the students as
he was with his congregation at the Princes Street
Mission in Barry', and described the tutor as, 'Good-

looking, racy in speech, bright, witty and versatile.'[16] In the Evangelism classes he taught the students to be simple in their preaching, how to be topical and how to apply the message which included a direct appeal to receive Jesus Christ as Lord and Saviour. In the Church History classes he would often lay aside the straightforward lecture; for example, when dealing with the early Councils he would have two students to criticize their decisions and two to defend them. After a thorough discussion a vote would be taken. Although, during this period, students were expected to attend Luchana Mission, many of them would sneak away to hear Ivor Powell at Princes Street.

Very different was Glyndwr Davies, who had shared with Mr Fidler the pain of leaving Porth, and the joy of beginning afresh in Barry.[17] He was from the Welsh valleys, had a slight deformity in his lip, but his earnest manner presented his deep convictions very forcibly. Unlike Ivor Powell, Glyndwr Davies read all his lectures on Christian Missions and Heresies, which did not go down well with the students. They were also expected to write out in full all the lectures. No one, however, doubted his knowledge and zeal. His experience and faith are expressed in his favourite hymn, 'At peace with God, how great the blessing', from *Hymns of Consecration and Faith*. He could be absent-minded and on one occasion put the alarm clock on the doorstep and took the milk bottle to bed. In 1938 another former Porth student joined the staff. The Rev. Fred Legge had ministered in Rock and Presteigne in mid-Wales and came to Gabalfa, Cardiff in 1938. He addressed the School on the 7 March and the Log Book recorded

for 14 October, 'Rev. F. Legge commenced lecturing
in Church History. God willing he will take the subject in future'.[18] He was closely associated with the
Christian Missionary Alliance and the centre which
they opened a little later at Penarth. He married a
daughter of Mr T. Knight Jenkins.

The other lecturers during this early period were,
George Cole, 'clerical Cole', who taught English
Grammar, the Rev. Victor Thomas and the Rev. W. H.
Hughes. Mr Hughes was a Londoner who had been
converted while in the Royal Navy.[19] After being
trained at Spurgeon's College he went to Launces-
ton, Cornwall, came to Stanwell Road Baptist Church,
Penarth, and in 1937 started as a visiting lecturer at
the School.[20] At Barry he took the Greek text of Ephesians and helped with practical evangelism. W. H.
Hughes had a gift for personal work and would take
the students down to the Labour Exchange where
queues of men would be standing, start a conversation with some of them and then leave the students to carry on with the work. He established a
close relationship with each student and was always
ready to listen and advise. The students believed that
no one could utter the name of Jesus as he did. Students struggling with Greek, and there were a few of
them, must have been encouraged with Mr Hughes'
approach to that language. He would emphasize that
he was not trying to make scholars of them but
wanted to give them the key to the cupboard so that
they could go there and find what they needed.[21]

Unlike Mr Hughes and Mr Legge, the Rev. Victor
Thomas was not a denominational man, but was
pastor of the Evangelical Mission in Aberdare, which

settled down after a few years as Emmanuel Evangelical Mission in Bell Street, Trecynon, on the outskirts of the town. It was on the 28 September 1939 that, the 'Rev Victor Thomas of Aberdare commenced giving lectures on the Bible Doctrine of Salvation'.[22] He later went to work in South Africa. The other addition was Jim McHaffie, who stayed on to take care of the Bible House and act as secretary of the School.

Mr Fidler was in charge of all aspects of the work, and there was no committee or council which met regularly. He was the Honorary Principal and Mr Courcy Hamilton was the President of the School. There was, however, a group of referees, which shows clearly the missionary outlook of the School: H. E. Alexander, Esq., Ècole Biblique de Genève; Brig. Gen. F. D. Frost, C.B.E., Central Asian Mission; Rev. E. E. Grimwood, Director of Central Asian Mission; Miss E. M. Leathes, Wembley; B. Matthews, Esq., Parkstone; Rev. E. J. Poole-Connor, Sec. North Africa Mission; Miss Ruth Paxon, CIM; Miss B. M. Stephens, Cardiff and Rev. Jesse Sayer, D.D. [deceased].[23] Those near to Mr Fidler, in terms of friendship and geography, were Mr Courcy Hamilton and Miss Stephens. The Principal also had a close relationship with Mr Alexander and the Rev. Poole-Connor, while there were family ties between Courcy Hamilton and the Matthews family.

Within the sacred walls

References have already been made to aspects of the course, but more details are given by a student of the early period. It consisted of Biblical Analysis, covering the sixty-six books of the Bible, Introduction to Theology, New Testament Greek, Church History, History of Christian Missions, Polemics, Homiletics, Pastoral Studies, Evangelism, the English Language, and courses were also available in French, Bookkeeping and Voice Training.[24] There was some flexibility regarding the Greek, which was much appreciated by some of the students. The two main emphases were the knowledge of Scripture and practical application in terms of evangelism. Some new aspects were introduced occasionally as happened, according to the Log Book, in 1937:

5 October. Home Nursing Classes were commenced today, the tutor being Mrs Cross of Crogan Hill.

3 March. We commenced a Carpenter's Class this afternoon making trays for potatoes.

There was no report on progress made, but one practical area which did bring forth much fruit was the gardening, thanks to the expertise of Arthur Menthonnex, one of the students.[25]

From May 1936 until July 1938, 32 students were educated at the School of Evangelism, 1 from France, 1 from Switzerland, 6 from Northern Ireland, 11 from England and 13 from Wales.[26] One of the 1936 students, Stanley Jackson, left the Mission in Bracewell, Skipton, in September of that year. He received varied advice from different people, 'Keep firmly on the grounds of Sovereign Grace, for there's nowt else worth having', while another sounded a warning, 'Do not trust the Welsh people, they are emotional and not really reliable.'[27] Stanley Jackson with his broad Yorkshire accent, shared a room with Wilf Chapman from Birmingham, Jim McHaffie from Northern Ireland, whose sister Wilf Chapman married, and Vernon Parfitt from South Wales. It is no surprise that there were a few problems of communication. They also differed in temperament as was naturally true of the whole School. McClelland, from Northern Ireland, was more emotional even than the bubbly, auburn-haired Gwyneth Phillips from the Elim Foursquare Church in Llanelli. Grace Wagstaff had a keen intellect, while Vernie Parfitt was always ready to give his testimony and dwell on his experiences.[28] There were denominational and doctrinal differences as well, and Presbyterians and Baptists had to remind each other continually that it is good and pleasant for brethren to dwell together in unity. Denominationalists and Free Missioners had to understand each other, and concentrate on the fundamentals of the gospel, rather than on secondary matters.

Deep consternation was felt when the continental Sunday was introduced within the sacred boundaries of the School. Arthur Menthonnex, from Switzerland, dared to clean his shoes and do some gardening on a Sunday.[29] Different attitudes towards examination could be a bone of contention. On one occasion Stanley Jackson was upset:[30]

I am un-nerved today after a fierce discussion with one of the students about examinations. He maintains that those who study hard for tests are doing it for their own glory. I disagreed with him and the sparks flew.

Mr Fidler knew his students well. He realized what were the possible tensions that could be experienced,

and continually emphasized the need for discipline
and unity.

All students had to be out of bed at 6 o'clock in
the morning and were allowed thirty minutes to
wash, shave and make their beds. Everybody was
expected to spend thirty minutes in prayer and private
meditation, gather together for a further thirty minutes of worship, fulfill various duties, by which time
they were ready for their breakfast, prepared by
some of the students under the supervision of a
member of staff. Other duties had to be performed
before lectures began at 9 o'clock, continuing until 1
o'clock. Some afternoons were free, but most of them
were spent in visiting homes, the ships in the docks
and holding open-air services. A few lectures were
held in the evening, followed by private study supervised by a member of staff. A task, not sought by the
students, was that of lighting the three coke stoves,
'It was both a dirty and delicate job, because the fires
were regulated according to the draught placement
and both students and staff had a habit of tinkering
with them causing not a little friction at times'.[31]

The students were much more ready to respond to
the encouragement they received to decorate their
rooms, while it was a warning they received as far as
the old-fashioned gaslights were concerned, Mr Fidler
being a stickler for economizing, reminding the students that the gas should be kept as low as possible.
After all he was running the school on a shoestring.
On one occasion a student thought that he had turned the gas off in his bedroom, but, actually, he had
turned it up, and then went to bed. The rush of gas
had put out the light and the room was filled with

gas. Providentially, a room-mate returned to the room and was able to deal with the situation, otherwise the evening could have been fatal for the student in his bed.[32]

Not only did the students find Greek difficult but English Grammar as well, taught, after Mr Cole left, by Mr L. J. Todd. Singing, however, was a different matter. The lessons, taken by Mrs Fidler, would have been an entertainment to watch as she tried to teach those who had no idea of tone and time, one of them, at least, being tone deaf, singing one note all the time. There were, however, some exhilarating songs used in worship, brought over from the Geneva Bible School and translated from the French by Mr Fidler.[33] In the collection he included some of his own, at least one by Miss Stephens and a few of the established hymns by Isaac Watts and Charles Wesley. There was also a composition which was regarded as a School hymn, and Englishmen, Irishmen, Swiss and the French joined with the Welshmen to sing it lustily:[34]

God save the Principality; Restore the heavenly song,
The Cross of Love and Victory, Shall triumph over wrong.
God save the Principality; Revive each wand'ring heart,
Come Holy Spirit mightily, Thy searching light impart.

There's a new day dawning; There's a new day dawning,
Then arise ye men of Wales, Obey the Master's call;
There's a new day dawning; There's a new day dawning,
Send the light throughout the land, And crown Him Lord of all.

Singing was an obvious delight in the School.

Staff and students never lost sight of one of the main aims of the School, that of evangelism, and realized that before this work could be carried on faithfully and effectively, they would have to be much in prayer. The Diary of Stanley Jackson, already referred to, reveals the importance of both aspects, at the School and at Luchana. A few of the extracts will be included:[35]

We had a fairly good time, but not as good as ours at the Gospel Hall. There are two students who think that it is a sign of spirituality never to participate audibly in prayer. They tell us that Evan Roberts in the Welsh Revival seldom prayed in public but poured out his soul in private.

What a time we had in prayer tonight. The prayers were just wonderful, no more had we long pauses and strained feelings as before. We did not need to sing choruses in order to start prayers.

Jim and I have some blessed times in prayer in our own bedroom. We meet around the Word each evening and we are learning much more as to what prayer really means. We avoid vain repititions and worn-out phrases before the throne, and we get down to the things that really matter.

The emotion could be intense at times, especially when one or two particular students took part. Referring to one of them, Stanley Jackson commented on one occasion, 'I was afraid for him, for at one point his prayer became so intense that he fell to the ground groaning'.

It was in prayer that the students were quickened and strengthened by the Holy Spirit. Many of them would refer to a particular experience of being filled with the Spirit, but all were agreed that they needed supernatural power, whatever the differences might be as to how the Spirit was received. Stanley Jackson experienced the reality of God's presence in preaching at Luchana in January 1937:[36]

About two o'clock this Sunday afternoon Mr Fidler asked me if I would take the service at Luchana this evening. His voice was giving way and he had fits of coughing. I promised to do so. We had a wonderful time in the meeting, I cannot describe it. I have never felt the urge and compulsion of the Spirit of God quite like it. Souls were striken down and the prayer meeting which followed was one I shall remember for years to come. Conviction of sin was so real we all wept. We started singing, 'Would you be free from your burden of sin?', and a man got up and in broken tones confessed his sin and cried for forgiveness and was saved. The text was Joshua chapter seven verse eleven.

Reaching the lost

Evangelistic work in Barry itself was carefully organized, students being given a 'parish' to cover. After private meditation, lectures and dinner:[37]

We had a talk on personal evangelism and immediately afterwards we were sent to our 'Parishes'. Mine is in Church Street. We only had one hour and were given seven tracts so it wasn't the amount of work that counted so much as the thoroughness with which we did it. It took me one hour to do seven houses and I found a good reception at almost every door.

Every visit was not so encouraging, and the same student relates a different experience:

After dinner I went with Jim to visit the coloured man's colony in Barry Dockland. I got in contact with a man who was a back-slider and is now immersed in a gambling fever. He told me of his home in Africa where his mother had taught him about the things of God. He then came over to Wales and went into a Chapel in Barry Dock and soon discovered the hollowness and the sham of a formal religion. He graphically described the home in his own country where in prayer they used to cover their faces and cry to God. He equally graphically described the Parson in the Chapel in Barry. His eyes rolled and waved his arms furiously and he screamed, 'Take the beam out of your own eyes before you attempt to pull the mote out of another. Evangelize your own land before you go elsewhere'. I was terrified, I left him and departed from that little room up a flight of stairs and vowed that by the grace of God I would do whatever I could to win the heathen in England before considering evangelising in any other land, or amongst any other people.

On another occasion the students spoke to some men from Jamaica and they responded in exactly the same way as the African which Stanley Jackson met.

Every Sunday morning the students went, two by two, to the Docks, one carrying a small case of Portions and Gospels, and the other carrying Bibles and New Testaments. They would return begrimed with coal but happy to have shared the gospel and distribute the Scriptures. The Word of God was taken to the Barry and Cardiff Docks in thirty different languages, and one of the workers was able to report, 'Since this work commenced a little over a year ago 3754 portions of the Word of God have been given free, and 158 New Testaments and 48 Bibles sold to those doing business on the great waters.'[38]

Reception could vary from a warm welcome to a refusal to board a ship. There was an encouraging response when the witnesses talked to a man from Barcelona. He was unhappy because he was separated from his family but would not dare return to Spain because of the trouble in that land. He was helped to believe the gospel and trusted the Saviour. He gave all his money, 8½ pence, for a little, blue-bound Spanish Testament. It was men only as far as work on the Docks was concerned, because it was regarded too dangerous for the ladies to visit that area. Once, however, the ladies were given permission to go with the men, and one of them remembers the fright she had when a cabin door was slammed in her face. An example of what could happen was the experience of one of the male students when he visited a Russian ship. A sailor held him by the throat and cried, 'If you were in my country I would kill you'.[39]

Open-air service at Barry Island sands, 1938.
From left to right: Wilf Chapman, W. Austin, Jim McHaffie, Maureen Helen Strange, B. S. Fidler

Open-air services were held regularly during June and July 1938. Eight meetings were held during June, and the activity continued during July, with

the entry recurring, 'Gospel Service on the Sands at
Barry Island'. Another place of meeting was King's
Square in the town, where the students met with
their friends in the area to bear witness to the gospel.
One of the team referred to the example from Scripture which inspired them: 'The impelling force behind our Open-air witness has been the example of
Ezra as recorded in Neh. viii, and the consequent religious, political and social changes which followed.'[40] It was the desire of all concerned with the
witness that the Word would be blessed in such a
way that lives would be changed, bringing forth
fruit, not only in their own lives, but in their communities as well.

There was a slight difficulty during one period in
1939, when the Barry Urban District Council refused
permission to sell and distribute Scriptures on Whitmore Sands.[41] They agreed, however, to receive a
deputation from the School of Evangelism, and Mr
McHaffie was allowed to appear before the Park's
Committee. Some of the councillors were concerned
on many accounts, that the School was making a
profit, that students would preach to those who
wanted to enjoy themselves and that there would be
a breach of the peace. A thorough discussion resolved these problems. It was agreed that Scriptures
would be sold from baskets, when requested, and
that the students could visit Whitmore twice a week.
McHaffie assured the Committee that no profit was
being made, as Bibles were sold at the cost price of
1s.3d, and the 9d asked of children was below cost
price. The students made full use of their two weekly
visits.

The following year Jim McHaffie made quite sure that he had the necessary authority to visit the sands, and obtained the appropriate certificate from the police:[42]

Glamorgan Constabulary
Form of Pedlar's Certificate

In pursuance of the 'Pedlar's Act' 1871 I certify that James McHaffie of the School of Evangelism Cadoxton in the County of Glamorgan is hereby authorised to act as a Pedlar within the United Kingdom for a year from the date of this Certificate.

Age 24	Certificate 5 February 1940
Height 5'-7"	Henry James Superintendent
Complexion Fair	For Lionel Lindsay
Eyes Green	Chief Constable
Hair Brown	

Jim McHaffie was one of the regulars in the open-air services, joined by David Cave, Wilf Chapman and W. Austin. They formed a very effective team and would spend part of the long vacation evangelizing on Barry Island where they had the support of the owner of the Rose Cafe, who was a member with the Plymouth Brethren. He welcomed the students and provided them with beds and meals.[43] The ladies were also zealous in the open-air witness, taking part by giving a testimony, reading the Scriptures and playing a musical instrument. They felt that they had a particular contribution to make when visiting a hospital. Sully Hospital was visited regularly, and here, and at other meetings, the singing of Gwyneth Phillips was much blessed of God.

Evangelism was carried on in Barry, in the town itself, the Docks, the sands, a nearby gipsy camp and in Lavernock. The entry in the Log Book for 15 July 1938, recorded that, 'Two students went to Lavernock Camp to commence Evangelistic work there.'[44] The Rev. W. H. Hughes managed to have permission to visit the Holiday Camp, and opened up a large sphere of witness.[45] The students were back again in 1939:[46]

This year again we had a tent at Lavernock, where three large fields are covered with the tents of those seeking to escape the restraints of city and home for a time. Two students have been living and witnessing there during the month of August, and many interesting contacts have been made. Bibles and Testaments have been sold and definite decisions registered.

Further afield, in conjunction with the Rev. T. W. Gregory Hopper, two students pitched their tents in the Cotswolds to bear witness to the gospel in that area. One student helped with the 'Hop-pickers' Mission' of Hereford and Worcester.

Visits were made to nearby churches, to co-operate in evangelism and to give reports of the work in different areas:[47]

4 October 1938. The students went by bus to Cardiff to a meeting arranged at Gabalfa Bap. Church and four of the students spoke of the work at Lavernock, the Cotswolds, on the Sands and on the Ships.

Independent Mission Halls were visited, two in Cardiff, one in Aberdare and the Baptist Mission in Ystradmynach:[48]

11 July 1939. The Students went to Ystradmynach by car for house to house visitation, open-air witness and a Service in the Baptist Mission.

For all aspects of evangelism it was of the utmost importance to have Scriptures at hand to be given freely or sold. A small Bible House was formed to stock the Word of God in different languages. Much help was received from the Association for the Free Distribution of the Scriptures, the President, Rev. E. E. Grimwood, being on the panel of Referees of the School of Evangelism.[49] With such help it was possible to be more effective. A report of the work was issued in March 1939:[50]

Since the commencement of the School year on September 25 last, when we became officially affiliated with the 'Action Biblique' with Headquarters at Geneva, we have distributed 126 Bibles, 162 NewTestaments, 1966 Gospels and 2193 other portions in 29 languages on the ships; and 24 Bibles, 54 New Testaments, 276 Gospels and 386 other Portions in house to house visitation, and added to these figures are 146 of the special S.G.M. 'My Own Bible' for Sunday school children. These are paid for by the children, by a card system whereby the children bring pennies until the amount is paid in full. Thus our grand total from September 25th until Feb. 28 is 296 Bible, 226 New Testaments, 2242 Gospels, 2579 Portions.

Being affiliated with 'Action Biblique', the School was linked with a Bible House which worked with similar centres throughout the world, including Paris, Barcelona, Brazil and the Argentine.

Overseas connections

The reference to Geneva is a reminder of Mr Fidler's interest in the continent of Europe. He had personal and linguistic links with France and Switzerland. The most important was with the Bible House and

College in Geneva and Cologny, respectively. The relationship concerns Wales in general and Mr Fidler in particular. The story can be traced to the Revival of 1904–05 in Wales. Mr Anderson of the BTI Glasgow, visited Wales during the Revival and was deeply influenced by what he witnessed. On his return to the Institute he was instrumental, under God, in creating a spirit of seeking the Lord for revival. One of the students, Hugh Alexander, had been converted at the age of seventeen when visiting an aunt in Cologny, Switzerland, and when Mr Anderson returned from Wales, the student was quickened in spirit, which led on to what he described as the fulness of the Spirit. In the power of this fresh blessing, he, and others campaigned in Belfast, and Hugh Alexander himself felt strongly inclined to work overseas. He applied to the Church of Scotland, but before receiving a reply, returned to Switzerland, where he had been converted, spending some time in preaching in Switzerland and France. He became aware of the desperate need of the gospel in both countries, and as he had, by now, been turned down by the Church of Scotland, the young preacher decided to stay in Switzerland. In 1917 he opened the 'Bureau des publications de l'Alliance Biblique', roughly a hundred metres from the present location, 11 Rue de Rive, in the heart of the city of Calvin. In 1925, the name was changed to 'Maison de la Bible' (Bible House), moved to its present premises in 1926 under the name 'Action Biblique'.

Hugh Alexander was also interested in starting a Bible School so that he could send out men to preach the gospel as well as sending them to distribute the

Scriptures. The Word of God should be read and pro-
claimed. He made a small beginning and in 1928 the
Geneva Bible School was inaugurated.[51] Mr Fidler
must have been in contact with Mr Alexander since
the Porth days, and after moving to Barry the link
was strengthened by visiting each other. When Mr
Fidler visited the Bible School at Cologny in 1938, he
also attended the annual conference held at Isenfluh,
Switzerland.

The two men were kindred spirits. Both of them
deplored the havoc created by modernism, held the
theological colleges mainly responsible for it, both of
them were committed to Bible teaching and had a
longing to see God at work again in revival terms.
The two men believed that the Revival of 1904 was
of God and were unhappy with the growth of Pente-
costalism immediately after the Revival, especially
the emphasis on tongues.[52] Both principals believed that such a movement was proving counter-
productive. The need they argued, was for a humbling
work of God's Spirit, which should be sought fer-
vently in prayer. As in Cologny, there was a Friday
night prayer meeting at the School in Barry, to pray,
not only for the needs of the School, but for those of
the whole world, and to plead with God for those
promised showers of blessing. Mr Alexander invited
the friends of the Bible School to this meeting, as Mr
Fidler did at Barry, and although the number of
friends attending at Barry decreased, the prayer
meeting continued until 1985.

The first reference to Geneva in the School books
was on 10 April 1937, when Arthur Menthonnex of
'Le Roc', Cologny, Geneva, was accepted as a student.

During his stay representatives of 'Action Biblique' visited Barry:[53]

10 May 1938. Visit of Mr H. E. Alexander of the Ècole Biblique de Genève, accompanied by Mme Berthoud, M. Philip Berthoud and Mlle Wyss. Mr Alexander spoke to the students and others in the afternoon.

Mr Alexander based his message on Acts 1:8, taking a person's home country as Jerusalem, and the surrounding countries as Samaria and Judea. Failure in Samaria and Judea meant that the gospel had not been taken to all parts of the world. Arthur Menthonnex was ready to leave in June 1938 and on behalf of the School Stanley Jackson presented him with a Bible. Mr Hatten of Penarth read the Scriptures, and the speakers represented the students and the Central Asian Mission. Arthur was leaving for his home in Switzerland prior to leaving for Central Asia. Arthur was followed by Jean Steudler from Neuchâtel, Mr Fidler accepting him free of charge as long as he paid his fare and promised to help in the College. During his stay Jean-Louis Steudler made ten chests-of-drawers for the students' rooms. [54]

Mr Fidler had a good command of French, and had long-standing contacts with France, one of the most important being that with Pastor M. Reynault, a pioneer worker in the country, who had established causes at Colombes, Paris and the Mulhouse (Alsace and Lorraine).[55] The Principal was also in touch with Madame Madelaine Charles, the wife of Professor Charles, both Roman Catholics, who lectured on discoveries relating to Bible history. She had sent a copy of her book to Mr Fidler, entitled, *Celui*

Qui Revient (He who will come), as she was convinced of the truth of Christ's second coming, which
would be personal and visible. The text, 2 Timothy
4:8, had played a significant role in forming that conviction.[56] Mr Fidler was glad to correspond with her,
and encourage her in the truth, one of the central
doctrines rediscovered during the Revival of 1904 in
Wales.

There was a three-way traffic as far as missionary
work overseas was concerned: missionaries visited
the School, overseas students returned to their native
country, and students from home and abroad went
to different countries throughout the world. During
the first year, 1936-37, representatives from nine societies and agencies were welcomed at the School:
European Christian Mission, Scripture Gift Mission,
World Evangelization Society, Sudan United Mission,
Unevangelized Fields Mission, Bolivian Indian Mission, Central Asian Mission, the Army Scripture Readers and the Bible House, Barcelona. An example of a
student returning to her own country was Martha
Helena Lamaroux, who returned to France and became the wife of Pastor Fritz Bühler, Mulhouse. [57]

Commitment and relaxation

From May 1936 until May 1939 there were 45 names
on the School Register. At least three of the students
from overseas went to work in a country other than
their own. The two Swiss students have been mentioned, and Rudolph Libek from Latvia became the
pastor of a Baptist Church in Scranton, Pennsylvania.
Of the home-country students only a few went to

work abroad, although three of the first seven did so. A few worked with missions and agencies at home, one with the YMCA, one with the London City Mission, one with the Billingsgate Medical Mission and one with the Irish Evangelistic Band. The 45 can also be divided geographically, 18 were from Wales, 13 from England, 7 from Ireland (6 from the North, 1 from Eire), and 6 from overseas. [58]

The School was a small one, with 17 students in May 1939. There was a homely atmosphere, with Mr and Mrs Fidler like father and mother to the students. As far as the course was concerned the emphasis was more on the practical, on the applied studies, rather than on the academic side. Some of the students did not have a basic education before entering the School, and had to be led on slowly and patiently in their studies. It was more complicated when overseas students arrived with very little English. Two of the home students had to teach one student, privately, and within six months he was able to preach in English. Many of the students felt the pinch financially, and one of them regarded toothpaste as a luxury.[59] It is no surprise that fees were very slow in being paid. The seriousness of the situation is fully realized when it is remembered that at this time Mr Fidler had no fixed salary, but lived from day to day. He had to discipline himself to have no thought for tomorrow. All the sacrifice was for the sake of training Christian workers, whatever their abilities and gifts might be. Although the emphasis was on preparing students for all kinds of Christian work, a good number turned out to be pastors. Those who went out to preach on a Sunday were not well paid, and sometimes, not paid at all. One of the students had to travel by train to Brecon, walk through the snow for a few miles to his destination, stay overnight, and found in the morning that no one turned up for the service. He had to make the same kind of journey back on Monday, but was not paid because he had not preached. [60]

Barry School of Evangelism building, 1939

It was thought that it was worth while to install a telephone 16 February 1938, and the first call was a request for a Bible in Welsh.[61] The telephone would, in due time, pay for itself. It is impossible to estimate the cost of rebuilding the School, or even repairing it, if it were damaged by fire. Providentially that did not happen, but staff and students did have a fright one evening:[62]

6 November 1938. We discovered smouldering joists in the morning and realized how God had protected the building and us from what might have been a disastrous fire. Evidently

some child had put a firework through a floor ventilator
from the outside—Nov. 5—when fireworks were being let off
in great numbers.

A major crisis had been averted.

Staff and students could enjoy lighter moments
and welcome times of relaxation. A lady student
from Pembrokeshire made a mistake when she used
gravy instead of coffee in preparing a drink for the
students and Mr Fidler. In spite of her grave error,
the following morning Mr Fidler called for his Pembrokeshire coffee. Trips were arranged for the students. Mr Hamilton would arrange for them to travel
by motor bus to St Nicholas, then to Llandaff Cath-
edral, Angelina Street Mission and prepare tea at the
Exchange, Cardiff, where he worked. On another
occasion Mr Hamilton wanted to thank the students
for helping with the decorating in the School in
preparation for Mr Alexander's visit. The reward
this time was a trip to Porthcawl and tea provided at
one of the cafes in that seaside resort.[63]

These are just some aspects of the life of the close-
knit community during the early days of the Barry
School of Evangelism. The peace of the place was
about to be shattered. Storms were brewing in Europe
and dark clouds gathering over Britain. During 1938
and 1939 Hitler entered in triumph into Austria,
Czechoslovakia and Poland. Mr Chamberlain's um-
brella and piece of paper had to be exchanged for the
shelter and the bomb.

REFERENCES

1. For the background, Donald Moore, ed., *Barry* (Barry Centenary Committee, 1984).
2. Reports in *Barry and District News*, during 1939, and commenting on 'Trinity Presbyterian Church', 'Coincident with the 50th anniversary of the opening of Barry Docks several churches in the district celebrate their jubilee this year', 7 April 1939.
3. Donald Moore, op. cit., 329.
4. 'Free Churches and Confessional', *Barry and District News*, 1 May 1936.
5. Ibid.
6. Ibid.
7. Notice in *Yr Efengylydd*, June 1936.
8. M. Edna Perkins, 'The Romance of 55 years old Barry Mission for Navvies', *Cardiff Times*, 6 April 1940. Geraldine Courcy Hamilton (nee Hodgson), born in Dublin, but the family had lived in Spain for some years, where the Hodgsons opened the 'Luchuana' Reading Room. Met Courcy Hamilton during a visit to Cardiff, and met later in Spain. Lived for a period after marriage at 'Ballymacoll' [name of the Hamilton home in Ireland], opposite Canton Rectory, and moved to Tyla Morris, Pentyrch, Mid Glam. Mrs Hamilton was active in the social life of Cardiff, 'A Welsh Social Worker', *Western Mail*, 1 May 1928.
9. 'Veteran Cardiff Solicitor', *South Wales Echo and Express*, 27 March 1940. Became related to the Matthews family when Beryl de Courcy, daughter of Cedric, Frederick's brother, married Stanley Matthews of the family of Matthews, Harlow, Essex, *Burke's Gentry* (London, 1937). Stanley and Beryl lived for a time in Harlow House, Barry.
10. According to Rev. M. Danks, Barry, as related to him by Miss B. M. Stephens; interview Mr and Mrs Danks, 14 December 1994.
11. 'Sons of the Prophets in Wales', *Life of Faith*, 8 September 1960.
12. Ibid.
13. Log Book, Evangelical Theological College of Wales, Bryntirion, Bridgend. Henceforth ETCW.
14. Register of Admissions, ETCW.
15. Ibid.
16. The Rev. Stanley Jackson, now living in Thorpe Bay, Essex, kept a Diary during his stay at the Barry School of Evangelism, and sent a most helpful account of that period to the author.
17. Stanley Jackson, op. cit.
18. Information from Mr A. T. B. Jones, Gabalfa, Cardiff, 18 October 1994.

19. Stanley Jackson, op. cit.

20. Information from Mr Colin Rees, Penarth, 15 December 1994.

21. Stanley Jackson, op. cit.

22. Information from Miss Griffiths, Trecynon, 2 October 1994, Rev. Malcolm Jones, Maesycwmer, 6 June 1995.

23. *Occasional Report*, April 1938. Bernard W. Matthews, related to Mr Hamilton, wrote the 'Foreword' to Mary N. Garrard's, *A Memoir* (Mrs Jessie Penn-Lewis). In 1928 Jesse Sayer published his *Alphabetical Studies of Holy Scriptures*, notice in, *A Witness and a Minister*, June 1928.

24. Information from Rev. Wilf Chapman, Bluntisham, Huntingdon, letter 22 February 1995.

25. *Occasional Report*, March 1939.

26. Register of Admissions.

27. Stanley Jackson, op. cit.

28. Ibid.

29. Ibid.

30. Ibid.

31. Ibid.

32. Ibid.

33. 'Barry School of Evangelism Hymn Book', a collection of 40 hymns. Mrs McHaffie's copy was examined; she is now living in Backwell, Bristol.

34. Stanley Jackson, op. cit.

35. Ibid.

36. Ibid.

37. Ibid.

38. *Occasional Report*, 1938.

39. Mrs McHaffie, interview, 6 February 1995.

40. *Occasional Report*, 1938.

41. Log Book, 30 June, 1 August 1939.

42. Mrs McHaffie, op. cit.

43. Ibid.

44. Log Book, 15 July 1938.

45. *Occasional Report*, August 1938.

46. Ibid., September 1939.

47. Log Book.

48. Ibid.

49. *Occasional Report*, April 1938.

50. Ibid., March 1939

51. 'Ysgol Feiblaidd Geneva', *Yr Efengylydd*, September 1937 and information reeceived from Mr John Alexander, son of Hugh Alexander, Institut Biblique de Gèneve, Cologny. Miss Valérie Fanguin, ETCW,

Bryntirion, studied at Cologny, and has helped with information
and translation from the French. When the Rev. Stuart Olyott, one
of the visiting lecturers at ETCW, ministered on the Continent, he
used to visit Cologny.

52. Information from the Rev. Ken Peel, Yeovil, interview 19 April 1995.
Mr Fidler's concern for revival is evident in his sermons and addresses, Noel Gibbard Collection, Bryntirion, e. g., Is. lix.2, 'Our
great need is God's people confessing their own sins, repenting and
putting away all that grieves Him in individual life and in Church
life. Then we may expect a revived Church to increase daily without
Campaigns and desperate efforts to keep the organised church
going. There will have to be some clearances in the temple when the
Lord comes in. In the Revival of 1904–05 some churches missed the
blessing because they would not obey the Lord in putting away sinful, worldly things, but those that repented and sought the Lord
with all their hearts were visited by the Spirit of God in revival
blessing and multitudes were added to the Lord and the name of
the Lord Jesus Christ was magnified and God glorified'.

53. Log Book; *Occasional Report*, 1938.

54. Register of Admissions; *Occasional Report*, 1938. When he left, Jean-
Louis Steudler became an officer in the Swiss Army, left from the
École Biblique de Genève for mission work in Cairo and Alexan-
dria, returned to Switzerland for a brief period, and then went out,
with his wife and two children, to the Republic of Central Africa,
letter from Jean Steudler, in French, dated 5 September 1995, kindly
translated by Miss Valérie Fanguin, ETCW.

55. 'Cenhadaeth Feiblaidd Ffrainc', *Yr Efengylydd*, September 1933; Mr
Fidler was the secretary for Wales.

56. 'Dros Dir a Môr', *Yr Efengylydd*, November 1936.

57. Log Book; Register of Admissions.

58. Register of Admissions.

59. Testimony of Mrs Baggs, Barry, 20 November 1994; Mrs McHaffie,
op. cit.

60. Stanley Jackson, op. cit.

61. Log Book.

62. Ibid.

63. Ibid.; *Occasional Report*, August 1938.

3.
War and Peace
1939-1945

It was a time of preparation in Barry. The town was busily responding to the threat of war. The ARP men were training enthusiastically and gasmasks were being distributed, 14,000 being issued on the first day of the appointed week.[1] In the School books there are reminders of the changes taking place. The German refugees at Glan-y-môr, Cold Knap, were visited by the students, who sang and spoke through an interpreter and distributed German Gospels. The following day Miss Moenich addressed the students and in the evening took Miss Strange, one of the School students, with her to Penarth and spoke in German to some Czech refugees.[2] Those who were far away from home must have been glad of friendship during this time of uncertainty, and of being able to communicate in a language which they could understand.

The foreign students in the School soon realized that the shadow of war was upon them. Miss Breslauer, a German, who was at the School for part of 1940, was taken by police to Bryn-mawr, while details of her person and stay in Britain were clarified. An Italian student, Lina Bernadicio Guerri, a converted Roman Catholic, preparing for the priesthood, spent 1939-40 at Barry. Trouble came when Mussolini declared war on Britain and France, 10 June 1940. Immediately after that date the Italians were rounded up, and within two days between sixty and seventy had been placed under detention by Cardiff police and about one hundred and sixty in Glamorgan. Guerri had to leave the School on the 10 June and was interred for a period, before being sent to Canada on the *Andora Star*, but he was drowned during the crossing. His body was brought back to Barry to be buried.[3]

Light in the black-out

As the war progressed the Principal had to be careful concerning the exemption of students from going to war, and had to be absolutely sure that everything was in order as far as the authorities were concerned. Two lady students, Miss Taylor and Miss Cooke, were summoned for an interview with the Ministry of Labour, in spite of the fact that they had been interviewed ten days earlier. A letter was sent from the School to the authorities seeking permission for the ladies to continue until the end of the intended term. The response was not recorded but it must have been favourable because the ladies continued in the School.[4] Visitors were also visible reminders of the war scene. Professor Martzinkovski, the archaeologist, not only spoke on 'Excavation in Palestine', but also related his experiences in a Russian jail. Jacob Vagar, a former Porth student, who visited the School, was later shot by the Russians.[5]

A few foreign students still entered the School. Erwin Ernst Jornot, from Switzerland, arrived just before the war broke out, and left before the end of

1940, leaving for home before going to work in South
America. By this time J. Steudler had also arrived
home in Switzerland, working as a supply teacher,
but hoping to work in Syria.[6] The bare reference to
'Mr Pokorny' hides a thrilling story:[7]

1 May 1939 Mr Pokorny arrived late in the day having been
allowed his passport & British Visa.

Augustus Erwin Pokorny was a German, living in
Austria.[8] His father was a co-founder of a small political party, the 'Left-wing Marxist Socialist Atheists',
and from an early age the son was indoctrinated
with the view that religion is the opiate of the people.
The parents separated and the mother sent Erwin to
a nunnery to be educated by nuns, an experience
which turned him against any form of religion. After
leaving the nunnery the young man joined the Hitler
Youth Movement. During 1933 Erwin was sent to
spy on some missionaries working in Austria. He
did so by attending classes to learn English, and the
textbook that was used was a German-English New
Testament. In this way he was introduced, not only
to the English language, but to the Christian message
as well. Indeed he could not avoid it as he was continually challenged by the missionaries to consider
the claims of the Lord Jesus Christ.

On one occasion the spy was nearly killed in a col-
lision between a motorbike and a car. Death became
a reality to him, and fear gripped his whole being as
he remembered words spoken to him previously by
one of the missionaries, 'It is appointed unto man
once to die and then the judgment'. He went to the

missionary, who was a great help to the anxious en-
quirer. Together they discussed Paul's conversion,
and studied a part of 2 Corinthians 5, concentrating
on verse 17, 'Therefore, if any one is in Christ, he is a
new creation; the old has passed away, behold, the
new has come.' Erwin went home and read that
chapter again, turning also to John chapter 3. He was
led to faith in Christ, and relates his own story: [9]

On the way home I thought deeply about it and realised that
to become a Christian I would have to undo what I had done
three years earlier at the Nazi altar in the Vienna woods on a
Whit Saturday, when I put my right hand on a Nazi dagger
on Hitler's book 'Mein Kampf', the new German bible, and
holding the Nazi flag in my left hand saying, 'At this holy
midnight hour I give my body, mind and soul to the Führer
Adolf Hitler'. After I returned home I read again John 3 and 2
Corinthians 5 and prayed that God would forgive me and
give me that new life in Christ. Becoming a Christian started
a lot of trouble in my life.

The young Christian had to respond to the fascist
regime of Dr Dollfuss in Austria, who was suppress-
ing all opposition parties and making use of concentration camps to silence dissidents. When Pokorny
refused to join the army and the Roman Catholic
Church he was imprisoned for a brief period.

Dollfuss was assassinated in 1934 but many problems faced Pokorny, and he decided to go to the
Ècole Biblique in Geneva to train for the Christian
ministry. In May 1936 he came to Britain and visited
Barry because Mr Fidler had invited him to spend a
holiday there. This was their first meeting and the
German must have been glad to meet Mr Fidler,
being delighted that they could converse together in

German. The visitor preached at Luchana from Philippians 3, verse 10, 'That I may know him, and the power of his resurrection, and the fellowship of his sufferings, being made conformable unto his death'. When Hitler invaded Austria, 13 March 1938, Erwin Pokorny was informed that he could not stay in Britain as he did not have a German passport, and he had to return to Vienna.

The Germans wanted Pokorny to be a spy in Russia, but he refused, and was appointed to be an interpreter of English and French in the Bomber Command. A former Hitler Youth leader told him that there were plans for him to be moved to the Gestapo, and the German Christian knew that he would have to leave Austria as he could not take part in their activities. He himself describes the situation:[10]

The British Vienna Embassy would not give me a visa, since I was not Jewish, and told me I would have to get an affidavit from a British subject inviting me to his home. I wrote to Mr Fidler asking him to give me an official invitation to study at Barry School of Evangelism, telling him, 'If I stay in Austria now part of Germany I must pledge my allegiance to the Führer. How can I do that when I have pledged my all to the Lord J.C.' On January 9th 1939 I got Mr Fidler's official invitation in English, French and German.

The prospective student left Austria on 3 April 1939, travelling across Switzerland, France and Belgium. He had some difficulty with the MI5 on his arrival, but eventually found his way to Barry, arriving on 1 May 1939. His future wife left Geneva on the day that war broke out, and although engaged to be married, the wedding did not take place until 1947.

Only about two months of the term remained when Erwin Pokorny arrived in May, and before restarting in September he spent some weeks working with D. M. Russell Jones in Exeter, who was an old Porth student and future minister of Gabalfa, Cardiff. The student was invited to stay on in Exeter, and was happy to do so, in spite of possible difficulties because of his nationality. Soon, however, he, like the Italian student, was in trouble and was interred again in 1940. [11]

The suffering of Dennis Edward Parry, a student during 1942–4, was rather different. He was brought up in South Norwood, London, the youngest of a family of six, and lost his mother when he was very young. After being converted at the age of twenty, Dennis attended the Keswick Convention in 1937 and responded to the missionary call made there in one of the meetings. When he was ready to apply to go to college, war broke out, but he was convinced that he could not take part in it. He took his stand as a conscientious objector.[12]

The problem with his call-up started when Dennis worked as a shop assistant. The first tribunal he attended in London on 2 March 1940 agreed that he should do land work instead of joining the forces. The conscientious objector refused to accept the decision. It is not clear what happened immediately after the tribunal because Dennis Parry was accepted by the Barry School of Evangelism in January 1942, but he had ceased to be a shop assistant in February 1941. Probably, Dennis believed that having finished in the shop and having been accepted by Barry he was free from doing land work. Before the end of

April 1942 he was again summoned to a tribunal, and the panel spoke sharply to him, reminding the objector that he was a shop assistant when the decision of the first tribunal was announced.

The Londoner would not be moved and told the panel that he had been called to the army of the Lord Jesus Christ with the aim of working in Africa. God had to come first, 'Without any doubt God must come first'.[13] After an adjournment the Bench announced their unanimous decision to sentence Dennis Parry to six months imprisonment. The stand reveals Dennis Parry's strong conviction and his determination to hold to it when in the minority. His views would not be those of the majority of the School, and just over a month previously Luchana had made a collection of £7 to support Winston Churchill's 'Aid to Russia Fund'. When he returned to the School, the conscientious objector was given a warm welcome by staff and students, irrespective of views concerning war and peace.

When he finished his course in Barry, Dennis Parry was accepted by UFM, and another person who was accepted by the same Mission was Nora, a girl known to Dennis from childhood days. They married on the field in the Congo (Zaire), and three of their four children were born in that country. Dennis loved the work of village evangelism and both of them, husband and wife, were responsible for a number of projects, especially the adult school that was set up with the purpose of establishing the Christians in the faith. Both are excellent examples of believers working quietly and faithfully without being mentioned in the headlines in any way. Nora had to persevere in her ill health and at one time had to be carried around in a chair.

During the time of the Simba rebellion Mr and Mrs Parry and two of their children were taken to Banalia, where, with another missionary family and three lady missionaries, they were placed under arrest. A party of mercenaries under Major Mike Hoare arranged to rescue the believers, and made the journey along the narrow and dangerous roads. They arrived at Banalia:[14]

The streets were empty, the houses were empty, the prison was empty. The mercenaries made their way to the river bank and near to the landing place of the pontoon they found an assortment of clothing which was both torn and blood-stained. There were two sets of women's clothing, three Roman Catholic nun's habits and one priest's habit, a shirt with a letter to Dr Sharpe in the breast pocket, two pairs of children's jeans and one tee-shirt belonging to Grace and Andrew Parry, two shirts with a 'Made in England' label on them, one having a letter addressed to an African in the pocket, four separate shoes, two women's, one child's and one indeterminate, Miss Baker's passport, Mr Parry's driving licence, Dr and Mrs Sharpe's identity cards and private papers and Miss Gray's identity card and Bible. The sight brought tears to the eyes of the hardened rescuers for they could only imagine the last hours of anguish suffered by the gallant band of missionaries.

Dennis Parry died during a period of bloodshed, and it must have grieved his heart to see the country torn in such a way, yet he knew that God had given him his heart's desire, which was to live and die in the Congo. To the natural eye he had been conquered but the spiritual eye could see him as one who had come out, victoriously, from the great tribulation. He was one of many who were faithful unto death during that period of persecution.

School group, 1945. *From left to right, front row:* Fred Legge, Glyndwr
Davies, Mrs Fidler, B. S. Fidler, J. W. Owen, F. S. Copleston.
Second row, second from right: Paul Tucker.

Nearer home, the links with St Athan's Air Force
Camp were strengthened. During 1939 Mr Allchin
from the School was active at the 5,000 strong camp,
with plans being made to increase it to 10,000. He
worked there two evenings a week and was thinking
in terms of being full-time as an Army Scripture
Reader, but when the war broke out he had to join
the armed forces. His place was taken by Mr Agnew,
the only one in the School qualified in terms of the
minimum age of thirty-eight years. Agnew was allowed to visit four times a week instead of the previously arranged twice a week. A further encouragement was the opening of a 'Rest Hut': 'On June 25

the ASR Hut, "The Airmen's Rest" was opened under the charge of Mr and Mrs Cirel and Mr Mills, and in the opening campaign by Messrs Montague Goodman and R. Laidlaw [staying at the School], seven or eight men accepted the Saviour. Please pray for the work in the Airmen's Rest, and also for Mr Watkins and myself as we proclaim the glad news inside the camp'.[15]

The war made a difference to the staff as well. Those present at the Staff Prayer Meeting, 10 November 1939, were Mr and Mrs Fidler, Rev. Victor Thomas, Rev. F. Legge and Mr McHaffie.[16] Mr Hughes had left to be a chaplain in the navy. A Londoner, trained as a blacksmith, Mr Hughes had a passionate love for the sea, but now instead of going to enjoy himself he was going to minister to those who were facing the storms of life and the waves of uncertainty. Before the end of the war one of the Reports reminded the supporters of those from the School who were in the war itself: [17]

The Following are in His Majesty's Forces:

Our esteemed Tutor, Rev W. H. Hughes, Chaplain in the Royal Navy.

Former Students:

Army	*Air Force*
G. W. McClelland	D. Cave
Vernon Parfitt	L. Stevenson
J. Aindow	
H. E. Penry	*Navy*
C. J. Meadows	I. G. Bartlett
P. Amies	
	Swiss Army
	J. L. Steudler

One of the visiting lecturers was Mr J. Hatten, M.P.S., Penarth, and he, his wife and his mother, had a frightening experience during the early part of the war. Mr and Mrs Hatten had decided to decorate a part of their home, and they moved the furniture into the front part of the flat. What happened is described by Mr Hatten himself:[18]

When the bombs fell they shattered the roofs and ceilings of the empty part, the ceilings remaining perfectly intact in the half covering our furniture - to the very inch; our home and stock unharmed. As wardens we had been told to stay at home and rest that night, but this was overlooked and our bell rang twice, so when the bombs came we were out on duty, our lives safe.

Two weeks later four bombs fell around my mother's house in the same town, three in her back garden. She and five others were in the house unharmed. In each case, mother and son, two houses next door were demolished, we escaping with roof, ceiling and window damage. So far from being 'a plague', our dwellings received 'first aid'. My mother's house is already rebuilt and our flat is soon to receive repair.

Cardiff and district and Swansea were hard hit during the period of war.

Conscientious witnesses

Death was not only an enemy from without, but from within as well. In the case of Mr Frederick de Courcy Hamilton, however, he knew as a believer that the sting of death had been taken away by his Saviour. Mr Hamilton passed away at his home, Tyla Morris, Pentyrch, on 27 March 1940, at the age of 84.[19] He came from Norfolk to Cardiff in 1873, but his father was from Ballymacoll, Co. Meath. Frederick Hamilton was articled to Mr Clement Waldron, and in 1878 was a partner in Hamilton and Hume. As a director of the Cardiff Exchange and Office Company he had influence in the sphere of trade and industry. Whenever there was a significant development in the town, he would encourage it, as he did with the formation of the High Street Arcade in Cardiff. He was also sensitive to the social and spiritual needs of the people of Cardiff. The Salvation Army were glad of his support, as were the navvy missions in Barry, Cardiff and Taff's Well. When R. A. Torrey came to Cardiff in 1904, Mr Hamilton acted as honorary treasurer.

Having such commitments it would seem that Mr Hamilton had no time for other activities, but that was not the case. He was keenly interested in amateur dramatics, and the one book which he wrote, *The Eternal Quest*, was illustrated by his own black and white drawings. That was not the only form of art that gave him satisfaction as he was also an amateur artist in colour. He regularly exhibited at the South Wales Art Society meetings, and for a period of time a number of his paintings adorned the walls of the Luchana Mission. That is not the end of the story because Mr Hamilton was zealous in his support of the Queen's Jubilee Nurses Institute and the NSPCC. Here was a man who could be found transacting business in the Exchange, worshipping at St Nicholas' Anglican Church, witnessing overseas, visiting the navvies at Luchana, arguing the case of the needy or relaxing at his easel.

After acknowledging the School's debt to Mr Hamilton regarding the beginning in 1936, because humanly speaking there would have been no beginning but for his generosity, the 'Obituary' in the *Annual Report* added some detail:[20]

His visits to the School which towards the end had become rather infrequent owing to failing health, were always appreciated both by Staff and Students. His personal interest in the individual students had gained for him a very warm place in their hearts and the news of his home-call created a sense of loss to us all. Sometimes he would give a very helpful talk in the Class-room, and the Students who were privileged to hear him will not easily forget his interesting addresses on 'Creation and Construction', and 'Architecture'. His keen love of the Lord and zeal in His service were an inspiration, and his gift for dealing personally with souls had brought many to the Saviour.

The obituary closed by giving thanks to God for a faithful warrior who was now at rest.

Mr Hamilton passed away in March 1940 when arrangements were being made to make the governing of the School more efficient. It was decided to form a School Council:[21]

The first meeting of the Council was held in the School on April 29th, 1940, at 2.45, when there were present Miss Stephens, Mrs Fidler, Rev. B. S. Fidler, Rev. G. Davies, Rev. V. F. Thomas, Mr T. K. Jenkins & J. McHaffie.

After the reading of 1 Chron. XXVIII 20, 21 by Rev. B. S. Fidler prayer was led by Rev. V. F. Thomas. The following appointments were unanimously made:

Chairman of the Council: Rev. B. S. Fidler proposed by Mr Jenkins, seconded by Rev. V. Thomas.

Secretary—J. McHaffie proposed by Rev. G. Davies seconded Rev. V. Thomas.

Treasurer—Mr T. K. Jenkins proposed by Rev V. Thomas seconded by Rev. G. Davies.

Besides those present it was announced that the following had also accepted invitations to serve on the Council: Rev. J. W. Owen, Cardiff; Rev. F. J. Legge, Cardiff and Rev. W. H. Hughes, Penarth.

Conditions of membership, duties of the Council members and the Basis of Faith were discussed. There must have been some difficulties with one clause of the Basis of Faith but they are not specified, and it is a pity that there is no more light on the matter. Eventually there was agreement on the wording: 'That as a consequence of the Fall human nature has become guilty and depraved, and the regenerating work of the Holy Spirit alone makes possible the exercise of saving faith in Christ for justification. Notwithstanding, those who remain impenitent are fully responsible for their wilful continuance in sin and unbelief.'

The Council of Reference did not change much in its composition. Compared with the list for 1938, only one name was added by 1940, that of the Rev. W. H. Aldis (CIM), another appointment in keeping with the world-wide vision of the School. The only other change was that by this time Bernard Matthews was in Bermuda. Most of them continued to visit the School occasionally.

In spite of difficulties, within and without, staff and students did their best to get accustomed to the black-out, and, eventually rations. Probably, the black-out was a greater challenge than the rations, because there was no fatted calf on the School menu even before the war. Full advantage was taken of the National Day of Prayer in 1940:[22]

26 May 1940 National Day of Prayer. We were able to hold a great Open-Air Meeting in the Amusement Park after the Sand Services. The owner had very graciously erected loud speakers and arranged a platform. There was a large attendance.

As mentioned in the entry, services were still held on the sands, and also on King's Square. The students were joined by others who desired to share the good news of salvation in the Lord Jesus Christ.

There were two notable characters among that company, Ted Sherwood and Jack West. Ted had been a welter-weight boxer and had won a Lonsdale belt, but after his conversion was on fire for the Lord, as was his friend Jack, whose main interest had been dog-racing. On one occasion Ted Sherwood was almost hoarse and asked a young student to take over. As he started to speak a WAAF in the front of a crowd of between four and five hundred, challenged the preacher, 'How do you know that there is a Jesus Christ?' The youngster prayed quickly and was given wisdom to respond. He questioned her, and she answered, 'What day is it?', 'Sunday.' 'What month is it?', 'June.' 'What year is it?', '1943.' The speaker explained to the challenger that everything makes sense when you begin with the death and resurrection of the Lord Jesus Christ. The word reached the heart of another person in the crowd, and he was converted seventeen years later and related the story to the preacher on that occasion. [23]

The young lad who took part in that open-air service was Ian Richard Kyle Paisley. His father, Kyle Paisley, Ballymena, was a personal friend of R. B. Jones, John Thomas and B. S. Fidler, and visited the School on 5 April 1940.[24] This link with Mr Paisley

senior accounts for some of the Irish students coming to Barry. It must have been a tremendous experience for the sixteen-year-old to come to Barry, especially to visit the Docks, and his Welsh friend, Clarence Meadows, was only a year older.

Servicemen would leave in the ships not knowing
whether they would return or not. Such uncertainty
made them more willing to listen to the gospel, and
to accept a Testament or a portion of Scripture. There
were some remarkable conversions during this period.
An example would be the experience of Clarence
Meadows and Dennis Parry when they went to the
Cardiff Docks. They met with two men leaving for
national service, one nervous at leaving, the other
person terrified. After some sharing and discussion
the four men went on their knees on the Docks and
cried to God, both servicemen confessing that they
had found salvation in Christ. When the students
looked at them they could see the change in the faces
of the two. It was a remarkable, immediate transfor-
mation.[25]

Another duty expected of the young man from
Ulster, and the other students, was fire-watching.
They would meet in Cadoxton School, where they
practised their billiard playing, and listened to the
young preacher from Northern Ireland as he shared
his sermons for the coming Sunday. Indeed, this
period in Barry was crucial for his future ministry.
He had been given a verse from Scripture, 'Follow
me, and I will make you fishers of men', but the
Devil was creating doubt in his mind. When the student came down to breakfast one morning, the reading was from the passage which contained the verse,

'Follow me, and I will make you fishers of men'. Co-incidence, the Devil whispered to him. They went in to morning worship, and the hymn was based on the words, 'Follow me, and I will make you fishers of men', including the first verse:[26]

> Boats and nets they left behind
>   Those disciples by the lake,
> Christ to follow, He would teach them
>   Men alive henceforth to take.

The young lad knew that this was no coincidence, but confirmation from God. There was no turning back now. He could face the future with confidence and prepare himself as much as possible for that most high calling of a preaching ministry. To quote the big man himself, 'I cut my preaching teeth at Barry. Northern Ireland is responsible for everything else.'[27]

The visitors to the ships were very encouraged with the response as they witnessed a marked change in the attitude of the men at the Docks. The Norwegians who had been so indifferent were now seeking portions of Scripture, and the French, who always complained that they had no money, were regularly buying Testaments or Portions. When a bomb damaged a ship in the Docks a salvage vessel was sent to help, and the students managed to sell two Bibles on board. As one of the workers commented, 'Hitler has been helping to increase our sales.'[28] During that same year the students changed their method; while previously Bibles and Testaments were sold and Gospels and Portions given freely, they decided to sell all Gospels and to give Portions only after a personal talk. In the light of this change the distribution was quite remarkable, because, from September 1939 to July 1940, 641 Gospels were sold and 1,604 Portions were given to interested people.

Visiting the Docks in Cardiff and Barry, The Sailors' Rest, The Soldiers' Billet and Sully Hospital needed a constant supply of Scriptures, and, consequently, renewed attention was given to the Bible House. Plans were made to expand, and, on 6 February 1940, the enlarged and improved Bible House was opened by Miss B. M. Stephens. Mr McHaffie was responsible for the running of the centre and continued in that capacity until 1942:[29]

27 November 1942. At the Prayer Meeting this morning a presentation of a complete set of Matthew Henry's Commentaries was made to Mr McHaffie who is taking up the pastorate of two Baptist Churches—Cefn Hengoed and Penybryn, and therefore relinqishing the management of the Bible House, though still retaining connection with it.

The work was left in the capable hands of Mr and Mrs Fidler.

There was continuing encouragement as far as the Bible work was concerned, as is revealed in the report for 1944:[30]

17 October 1944. The a/c's of the Bible House were next considered. Mr Williams, one of the students was to give a report of these. This report covered the two years from July 1942–June 1944. In the year 1942 there was a net loss of £19. For the year 1943–44 the sales were £945, gross profit £178; net Profit £200 with Capital at £407. There was £132 in the Bank. Sundry Debts amounted to £69.

At the same meeting the remuneration for Mr and Mrs Fidler for their work in the Bible House was considered, and it was agreed to pay them £1 a week retrospectively.

It was possible to walk in order to take the gospel and the Scriptures to various parts of Barry, but difficult to travel to other areas because petrol was scarce. One way of overcoming the difficulty was by using a caravan, which could cover a wide area quickly, and petrol would be allowed for travelling to preach. Mr Fidler introduced the matter to the Council on 15 May 1941. He informed the members that Mr Evans, Pontypridd Road, Barry, had a caravan which he would be glad to dispose of for evangelistic purposes, and it was agreed to buy it. At the same meeting Robert Rowland's willingness to be a School evangelist was considered, as he was convinced that God was calling him to that ministry. The Rev. Victor Thomas had spoken to him and was sure that Robert Rowland was the right man for the work. In response to this report the Rev. Legge proposed, Rev. Thomas seconding, that the student should be appointed as School evangelist. He was to concentrate on working from the caravan, and, in their turn, the students would join him in order to gain experience in evangelistic work. Terms agreed on were £1 per week, plus expenses, but in the next meeting this was changed to £1.10s.0d. to cover all expenses. [31]

The work of caravan evangelism started almost immediately after the end of the School year:[32]

16 July 1941. Public gathering at 'Luchana' in the afternoon addressed by Mr Spencer Johnson. After this there was the public dedication of the Gospel Caravan 'Le Roc' when Rev. Geo. Banks gave a short appropriate address.

The following day the caravan was towed to Hay-on-Wye.

The launching of the caravan was the beginning of demanding pioneering work for the evangelist and the students who supported him. Hay presented a challenge, but there was encouragement as there was an evangelical witness in the town. The beginning of the cause reveals the tension that could arise within a denomination. One of the Jeffrey brothers had visited the place, and under his ministry a lady had been converted, but when she went to her home church she found that there was no welcome for her. She found fellowship with a few other believers and the Mission was started in Hay. When Robert Rowland went there he worked with the Mission and within twelve months was invited to be the pastor. He responded positively, and it is a matter of interest that the Mission is pastored today by the husband of a former student.[33] As he was a pastor Robert Rowland could not continue as car-evangelist, and arrangements had to be made for someone to take his place.

The student who was ready to fill the breach was Harold Edgar Lewis from Risca, Gwent. He was a serious, dedicated student, highly regarded by staff and students, but he could enjoy a moment of relief.[34] One such moment was to wait for a student to walk through the door and greet him with the sausage which was supposed to keep out the draught. On one occasion, however, it was not light relief, because it was Mr Fidler who entered the room and not a student. Edgar Lewis was willing to work for a while on the caravan before being recognized officially as car-evangelist. The caravan was in Builth

Wells and he joined it there for a brief period. He made a request to be set apart officially and Mrs Fidler travelled to Builth Wells to discuss the practical details with him. He was to start on £1.5s.0d. a week, which would be raised if help would be received from the district.[35]

One problem in working from a caravan was how to spend the winter months. Mr Lewis brought this matter to the attention of the Council, 3 November 1942, but as there was a possibility of receiving a call to a church, the matter was postponed. One need had to be dealt with immediately, that of heating the caravan, and it was agreed to purchase a stove. Mr Lewis moved to Talgarth, where he was greatly encouraged by the support of a local headmistress, Miss Williams. Meetings were arranged at her home in Llangorse, where she lived with her parents. Like Mr Rowland at Hay, Mr Lewis was invited to stay at Talgarth, and remained there for two years.

Other students joined in the caravan work. Fred Baggs concentrated on Rhayader, but was soon discouraged as there was very little response. A second caravan, named the 'Mayflower' was obtained, and was taken to Llanwrtyd, 'where Mr Ferguson & Mr Porter had been working with much success since July' (1942).[36] Robert Ferguson was a Scotsman, and later became a minister in the Church of Scotland at Motherwell, and then crossed to America taking an active part in the 'Word for Living' ministry at Knoxville. Derek Porter was from Thornton Heath, Surrey. He and his wife, a nurse, spent over forty years in Africa with the SIM, doing pioneering work and church planting, and for a number of years worked in a leprosy centre. When they retired in 1987 they settled in an SIM home in Sebring, Florida.[37]

The centre of activity at Llanwrtyd was the home of Mr and Mrs David Jones, both of whom had been converted in the aftermath of the 1904 Revival.[38] Their continuing witness to the gospel is an illustration of the lasting effects of the Revival, but living in a spiritually barren, rural area, they found it difficult to travel any distances in order to have good teaching. Such an experience is all too common in the story of those converted during and immediately after the Revival. According to members of the Jones family the chapels were fairly well attended but salvation was thought of in terms of good works. The few believers had to find some bread to satisfy their spiritual needs. They had the Bible, of course, read the works of Spurgeon and Christmas Evans, and followed regularly the sermons in the *Christian Herald*. The message of the students was sweet like honey to the believers but bitter herbs to those who opposed it. The latter were quick to point out that while so many young men were fighting for their country, the ministerial students were allowed to travel the country preaching the gospel. This tension did not make it easy for the missioners to win the ears of the Llanwrtyd people.

When the students arrived at Llanwrtyd to share the good news, Mrs Jones' comment was, 'They've got the real thing'.[39] She and her husband were glad to receive the evangelists because they could enjoy fellowship together and reach out to others in Llanwrtyd and district. The mission field included the home of the Joneses. There were seven daughters,

Flora the eldest having come to faith before the students arrived on 15 July 1942. During the month of August, Ethwyn Jones was converted, when she was fourteen years old. After Bible training at Swansea she spent twenty years as a nurse and midwife in Thailand. In that same month of August, Grace Jones, seventeen years of age at the time, came to a saving knowledge of the Lord Jesus Christ. Grace spent some time in nursing and caring, but died of cancer in 1971, after much suffering. Olwen, another sister, was away in Shropshire at the time, but was converted during a visit to the home in October 1942. She also had Bible training at Swansea before leaving for Damascus with the Edinburgh Medical Mission, and moved to a hospital in Bethlehem, where she is still working, but the hospital, because of developments on the West Bank, has been turned into a hostel. Jean Jones was the youngest of the family, and when she was eleven years old trusted the Saviour for salvation as a result of the faithful witness of many in the area. She was very conscious of the lack of teaching, and was happy to settle down in the Christian ministry when she married the Rev. Ira Mills in 1953.

The two other sisters, Edith and Mary were in the Forces. Edith was taken ill when she was in Hull, and it was during her stay there that she came to know the Lord, also in the autumn of 1942. She trained at Heightside, Lancashire, and left for the Lebanon with the British Syrian Mission. In 1956 she married Rev. Frank Mills, who ministered at Bedwas and Pengam, South Wales, and was Ira's brother. Mary was converted while stationed at Derby, as in the case of Edith, in the autumn of 1942. She later trained at the BTI, married Don Harries in 1952, and both left for Morocco to serve with the Southern Morocco Mission. The husband set up the radio work of the North Africa Mission, now known as the Arab World Ministries. The Jones family will remember 1942 for time and eternity. The family was made one, spiritually, and the providence and grace of God had been made manifest in a remarkable way. The students must have been humbled and lifted up as God blessed their ministry in that needy part of Wales.

Apart from the opposition they had to face, the students had, on one occasion, to deal with the distribution of undesirable literature in Llanwrtyd. Another problem was the lack of finance, as it cost ten shillings a day to keep a caravan. Some relief was gained by making use of the Missionary Fund as there were limited opportunities to support work overseas during the war period.[40]

A member of staff had supervised the caravan witness for a brief period but in 1945 the Council appointed Robert Rowland to be Superintendent of the Caravans, which meant renewing his link with that work, and, also, coming into closer fellowship with some former students. Many of them were in easy reach of each other. Edgar Lewis went from Talgarth to Pengam, Fred Baggs to Llanbradach and then to Cefn Hengoed, following Jim McHaffie. Baggs was followed at Llanbradach by Ivor Coleman, another former student, and according to the students of the day they had bags of coal in Llanbradach. Robert Rowland was enthusiastic concerning the work and

he could enthuse others as well. He attended to all
the details and kept a pastoral eye on all the workers. He came to the School regularly and one such
visit is recorded for 17 May 1945:[41]

Rev R Rowland spoke to the Students in the morning on the
work of the Caravans. In the Afternoon there was a Dedicatory Service when Miss Turner and Miss Rowland were set
apart for the Caravan work before going to Crickhowell,
there to commence Gospel work through the 'Mayflower'.

Laura Rowland was Robert Rowland's sister, and
she is an important link with the period after the
war, in terms of the Bible House in Barry and Colportage in South Wales.

Home and abroad

It was not possible to continue close relationships
with individuals and centres overseas. Some information would be received through the foreign students at the School: Rudolph Libek, Latvia; Ernst
Jornot, Switzerland; Irene Breslauer, Germany; and
Marie Blondell, Switzerland. Efforts were made to
keep in touch with 'Action Biblique'. At the beginning
of the Autumn Session, 1940, a message of greeting
was wired to Geneva, 'Thou shalt see greater things
than these'. A reference was made to this greeting
during the annual day in 1940, when, among the visitors, were Mr Laidlaw, New Zealand, and the Rev.
W. G. Stalley, Bournemouth, who was the guest
preacher:[42]

At both meetings the Students sang some of the songs translated from 'Songs of War and Glory' composed by Mr

Alexander, Principal of the Geneva Bible School, to whom a
telegram was sent earlier in the day assuring of our prayers
in the words of Psalm 34. Hence three other Bible Schools
were represented at our Annual Meetings: Geneva, in the
way indicated, the Auckland Bible School by Mr Laidlaw,
who is one of the Directors, and the B.T.I., Glasgow, by Mr
Stalley, who was a fellow student with Mr Alexander there.

The Council received welcome news from Geneva
that Jim McHaffie had been made a member of 'Action Biblique'. Mr Alexander was informed that they
were glad of the honour and assured him of their
prayers for the work in Geneva.[43]
    Prayerful interest in overseas work was inspired
by article and example. The 1940 Report included
an article by the Rev. Frank Evans, 'Win the War',
in which he acknowledged the Christian's duty to
Caesar, but, 'Our first loyalty must be given to our
Divine Commander'. He argued that duty to Caesar
should not prevent believers giving sacrificially for
the work of the gospel. He drew out a principle from
I Kings 17:13, to give to the man of God before meeting with our personal needs: 'The axe must be laid at
the root of our luxuries, not the missionaries' neces-
sities.'[44] If the nation was acting on that principle,
surely, the Church should do so. A shining example
was found in the life and death of Arthur Menthonnex. News of his death was received in June
1940, which brought forth many tributes from staff
and students. He had left in 1938, spent some time in
learning the Urdu language in order to work with
the Central Asian Mission in Kargil. He arrived at
that place and rejoiced in meeting some of his
friends from the Geneva Bible School. His period of

service was very short because he died of typhoid on 2 June 1940. Stanley Jackson paid tribute to Arthur's 'enthusiasm and determination', and ended the tribute by summarizing the debt which the School owed to him: 'The School today owes much of its usefulness to the influence of his life and testimony. He was one whom God called to blaze a trail and to lay foundations. The Bible Depot, the work on the Docks and the garden are all evidences of this. He laboured and others are entered into his labours.'[45]

Six of the students responded to the call to work overseas, one each with the Sudan Interior Mission, RBMU, UFM, and BMS, while the society of the other two is not mentioned, but, probably, one of them went to serve in Binar, India. One student worked with the British Jews Society at home, and a representative of that Society was present at the School on 16 May 1941. He was Mr Ernest Lloyd, who a few years later became a Council member, and at the time of writing is still faithfully attending the meetings, continuing to be a committed friend of the College. Representatives from other societies and bodies came to quicken the interest in different aspects of gospel witness, seven of them during 1940-41: ECM, LCM, Russia and Border State Mission, WEC, RBMU, Bolivian Indian Mission, UFM, and a student from Auckland Bible Institute. Even during the period of war the School managed to maintain the vision of the spread of the gospel throughout the world, not forgetting the field at home, both aspects of the witness helping each other.

Amidst all the changes of the war the staff at the School remained almost unchanged. Mr Hughes was

away on national service, and there was one addition
in 1944. A person who had visited the School on a
number of occasions was the Rev. W. E. Dalling, Sidmouth, Devon. He had worked in close co-operation
with the Rev. D. M. Russell-Jones, Buddle Lane, Exeter, both of them making a stand for the truth in that
part of Devon. Mr Jones recalls this time in Devon:[46]

Alas, it was here I clashed with the Denominational Authorities. With the Rev. W. E. Dalling, M.A., who later became a
dear friend, we took our stand against the conditions for
Ministerial Recognition. No one will ever know the price we
had to pay for our stand; we failed to see how that knowledge of Higher Critical views of the Holy Scriptures should
be the criterion of our fitness for the Christian Ministry.

Student group, early '40s

Mr Dalling had ministered in Southampton, but because of developments in the realm of ministerial training, he decided to leave the Baptist Union. He moved to Sidmouth in 1933 to pastor Emmanuel Evangelical Church which had just been opened a few months earlier.

Emmanuel had other connections with the School in Barry. It was from Mr Dalling's church that Idris Bartlett came to the School in 1942, and later in 1944, Joyce Page and Roy Russell, who became husband and wife. Roy Russell's parents had known Mr Dalling since the Ilfracombe days where they were brought up, and Mrs Russell's mother often welcomed D. M. Russell-Jones to Sidmouth and supported the work of Pastor Pokorny in Austria, when that started in 1948. Mr Dalling himself arranged a correspondence course from Emmanuel, and the School in Barry from its opening worked in collaboration with him, recommending the courses as suitable to meet the need of those who wanted to study the Bible systematically.

It is no wonder, therefore, that Mr Dalling was interested in the work of the School. He expressed his willingness to come to Barry as residential tutor. Mr Fidler was happy to proceed and assured the Council that Miss Stephens was in agreement:[47]

Rev Davis proposed & Rev Legge seconded that Rev & Mrs Dalling be welcomed heartily on the understanding that no financial responsibility was involved. This was unanimously passed. Rev & Mrs Fidler said they would wholeheartedly welcome Mr & Mrs Dalling.

Both were welcomed to the School on 24 March 1944,

with Mr Dalling acting as vice-principal, while continuing with his work as Principal of the School of Simplified Bible Study. The stay at Barry was short but not sweet. Tensions emerged between Mr Dalling and the students, and between Mr Dalling and Mr Fidler. Although one as far as the aims of the School were concerned, Dalling was completely different from Fidler in terms of temperament, and they had different approaches as far as the practical aspects of running the School were concerned. Fidler tended to be fussy about trivial things and Dalling, not without cause, tended to be impatient with him, but over-reacted at times. During the time of trouble some of the students were expelled and Mr Dalling resigned of his own accord, 'It was suggested that the joint principalship seemed unworkable.'[48] The Council decided to relieve Mr Fidler of all extra duties so that he could devote all his time to the principalship.

Echoes of the war were still heard within the walls of the School.[49] While home on leave W. H. Hughes paid a visit and spoke to the students at the dinner table. Mr H. G. Howell of the King's Bodyguard continued to come and Pastor Pokorny stayed for a brief period. The Rev. Caradoc Jones, who was working in Paimpol, Brittany, had met two Bretons during his time in concentration camp, and wanted them to come to Barry, but, probably because of financial reasons, this did not materialize. When faced with problems of war service, Mr Fidler could turn to the Rev. Blackmore, FIEC, as the School was affiliated to the Fellowship.

The students did find time for some recreation, especially walking and going to the beach in Barry.

One visit to the beach, which should have been a time of enjoyment, turned out to be a tragic one:[50]

21 April 1945. A very tragic day—Stanley Funnell went with some other students to Barry Island and, whilst bathing was drowned. On hearing the news Rev. F. J. Legge and Mr Howells (the King's Bodyguard), came.

A verdict of 'Accidental Death' was recorded and the body taken back to Hailsham to be buried, Mr Fidler officiating at the funeral.

The main concern of staff and students was for the spiritual health of the School, but that was not unrelated to the condition of the building. It was costly to run even without considering improvements, and nothing much had been done to improve it for a number of years. There was an obvious need for repairs and some paint. The need was discussed in one of the Council's meetings:[51]

The condition of the School building was first discussed. It was suggested that if outside doors & woodwork were painted a better appearance would be given to the building. One governing factor, it was stated, was that from August 1st only £10 could be spent on repairs. It was suggested that Mr E. Lewis be asked to do the work. Another suggestion was that paint should be used instead of distemper for inside decoration.

Very little could be done with £10 even in those days, but steps were taken to do some little things. A Property Committee was formed to work with Mr Fidler, comprising of Miss Stephens (convener), Mr Loveridge, Mr Copleston and Mr Willie, three of the four being added to the Council in recent years, although Mr Copleston was associated with the School from its inception in 1936. Mr Willie was a child of the 1904 Revival and one of the leaders in Minster Road Gospel Hall, Cardiff. His time of service was brief, while Mr Loveridge was just starting what was to be a long period of close association with the School. One of the priorities of the Committee was to provide a stove to heat the lecture room and when it arrived it must have been warmly welcomed by all in the cold building.

The Council also emphasized that there should be renewed efforts to establish discipline in the School. It was emerging slowly through a difficult period and it was important that care was taken not to undo the good work which had been accomplished after the time of tension. A further matter for consideration was Mr Fidler's financial support, as he depended on an honorarium from the Council, and this was supplemented by £125 per year.[52] The Annual Meetings, 4 July 1945, were times of blessing, and praise was the dominant note of the gatherings throughout the day, which began with the celebration of the Lord's Supper at 7 o'clock in the morning. At 9 o'clock David Cave presided over the Past and Present Students' meeting, addressed by Ernest Ridout. The Principal presided over the afternoon meeting, when reports were given of all aspects of the life of the School. The afternoon and evening preacher was the Rev. D. M. Russell-Jones, who preached in the first meeting on Acts 18:25, emphasizing the need for the unction of the Holy Spirit in Christian work, while in the other service, Mr Jones spoke from the Book of Revelation, chapter 12, stressing the need for holy, sanctified lives, if believers are to reach the throne. There were some grounds, therefore, for optimism after the close of the 1944–5 School year, and this was expressed in a hymn composed by Jim McHaffie for the Annual Meetings, sung to the tune 'Almsgiving'. After giving thanks to God for different aspects of the life of the School and his faithfulness during the war years, they looked to the future with confidence as they sang the last verse:[53]

> And for the future all unknown
> We put our trust in God alone,
> For He is still upon the throne;
> Our faithful Lord.

REFERENCES

1. *Barry and District News*, 5 May 1939.
2. Log Book.
3. Register of Admissions; 'Rounding up of Italians in Wales', *Western Mail*, 12 June 1940.
4. Register: Miss Cooke is on the list, but not Miss Taylor, however, she was staying at the School.
5. Log Book.
6. Register.
7. Log Book.
8. Information received from Pastor Pokorny himself, letters, 30 May 1994, 10 May 1995, copy of *Austrian Bible Mission* and copy of 'Testimony of Pastor Pokorny'.
9. Ibid.
10. Ibid.
11. Log Book.
12. 'Saved to Serve', in David Truby, *Congo Saga* (UFM, 1965), 79.
13. 'Conscientious Objector Sentenced at Barry', *Barry and District News*, 1 May 1942.
14. *Congo Saga*, (UFM), op. cit., 85.
15. *Report*, September 1940.

16. Information Mr Colin Rees, Penarth, 15 December 1994.
17. *Report*, 1944-1945; Wm Gordon and Henry Jones worked with the YMCA.
18. *Report*, September 1940.
19. *Burke's Gentry*, 1937 ed.; 'Veteran Cardiff Solicitor', *South Wales Echo and Express*, 27 March 1940; details of funeral, *Western Mail*, 30 March 1940; interview Mr and Mrs Danks, Barry, 14 December 1994.
20. 'To Be with Christ', *Report*, September 1940.
21. Council Minutes.
22. Log Book.
23. Tape: 'Reminiscence of incidents and students Barry School of Evangelism', Ian Paisley and Clarence Meadows.
24. Log Book.
25. Tape, op. cit.
26. Tape, op. cit.; interviews, Alun and Noel Gibbard, 27, 31, August 1994, 3 October 1995.
27. Interviews, op. cit.
28. *Report*, September 1940.
29. Council Minutes.
30. Ibid.
31. Ibid.
32. Log Book.
33. Information from Rev. Ben Illingsworth, ministering in Hay.
34. Tribute, interview Mrs Baggs. Mrs Dorothy Lewis, the widow, lives at Maesycwmer, in membership at Mount Pleasant.
35. Council Minutes.
36. Ibid.
37. Letter Derek Porter, 14 June 1995. He had experience with Fox's Mission, or Friends' Evangelistic Band, which came into being in 1919, as the result of the work of George A. Fox and the Friends' Prayer League. An account is given by Bessie Bryers, *To Them that Obey* (F.E.B., 1969); developed into the Fellowship for Evangelising Britain's Villages. Mr Brian Love, father of Andrew Love, former student at ETCW, Bryntirion, is involved in the work of the Fellowship in the south west of England.
38. Information received from members of the family, including interview with Mrs Flora George and Mrs May Harries at Aberystwyth, 4 July 1995, and letter with interesting information from Mrs Jean Mills, 3 July 1995. Mr Don Harris, May's husband, visited the College in 1957, 'M D Harris of the South Moroccan Mission gave a talk illustrated by film strip this morning', Log Book, 27 May 1957.
39. Letter Mrs Jean Mills, op. cit.
40. Council Minutes.

41. Log Book.
42. *Report*, September 1940.
43. Ibid.; Council Minutes, 22 January 1942.
44. 'Win the War', *Report*, September 1940.
45. Ibid., 'A Memoir'.
46. D. M. Russell-Jones Papers, ETCW, Bryntirion, Bridgend; informa-tion received from Mr and Mrs Russell, Sidmouth, interview 20 April 1995.
47. Council Minutes, 4 November 1943.
48. Ibid., 22 February 1945.
49. Log Book.
50. Ibid., and recollections of Mr and Mrs Russell, Sidmouth, who were present.
51. Council Minutes, 23 July 1945.
52. Ibid.
53. 'The Annual Meetings', *Annual Report*, 1945.

4.
Doubt and Faith
1945–1960

All was quiet on the western front and peace had been restored to the Barry School of Evangelism. Staff and students reminded each other that there is no respite in the spiritual warfare, as Satan refuses to take part in any negotiations for peace, 'No slacker grows the fight, No feebler is the foe', and human nature does not change. The tensions and dangers of war had passed away, but:[1]

The pleasure-seeking crowds have returned to Barry Island in greater numbers than ever, and the Fun Fair which was silent on Sundays before the war, is now in fuller swing than ever on Sundays. The places of worship, which ought to be filled with people gathered to thank the Lord for deliverance, are sparsely attended. The 'religion' of evolution which has had such disastrous results . . . as would shock Nero, is now broadcast to all our schools by the B.B.C. and the life of this nation is being poisoned at its source.

According to the same article, the description of Romans, chapter 1, verses 26 to 32 could be applied to post-war Britain.

Settling down and renewing links

Mr Fidler was still captain and marshalled his soldiers with the assistance of his officers. The Rev. J. W.

Owen, Heath Church, Cardiff, was appointed chairman of the Council in 1945,[2] and in 1946:[3]

12 Feb. It was resolved to invite Rev Rutt to the Tutorship to lecture on the doctrine of Salvation by Grace.

21 June. A welcome was extended by the Chairman to Mr Hughes on his return from his Chaplaincy in the Forces.

Mr Rutt was from Philip Street, Bristol, and Mr Hughes was returning to the School and to the church at Penarth.

The ranks were further strengthened in 1948. The Rev. F. S. Copleston, who had studied and lectured at Porth, and a Council member since 1944, was given the responsibility for teaching some Greek and Non-Christian religions. The Rev. Robert Rowland, a former Barry student and car-evangelist, began lecturing on the Doctrine of Salvation.[4] The third addition was the Rev. Read, who had found it impossible to return to India, where he had been working with the Central Asian Mission.[5] He was appointed as 'Temporary Resident Tutor' to help with lecturing and in the Bible House, where there was a real need at that time. Some attention had been given to it immediately after the war, and the need for a full-time worker was recognized. Help was received from a number of people but no full-time worker was found. Mr Read had a committee to support him, comprised of Miss Stephens, Mr T. Loveridge, Mr T. K. Jenkins and the Rev. Glyndwr Davies. There was an increasing demand for the cheaper editions of the Scriptures, and, soon, the stock was valued at £670.[6] Many of the colportage workers gained experience by working in the Bible House, going out to other centres and by establishing a relationship with Spurgeon's Colportage, which involved a number of Barry students, including Mr and Mrs Trevor Selway, R. J. Towler and Raymond Watts.[7]

Strengthening existing links with overseas countries and creating new relationships was a very slow process after the period of war. Only one student from Action Biblique, Switzerland, is mentioned.[8] The main contacts with the Bible House and the Bible School were the Principal himself and Ken Peel. During his last year at Barry, Ken Peel spent some months at the Llanbradach Baptist Mission, Mid Glamorgan, and from there went to Cologny for a period of twelve months, returning to Llanbradach before moving to Barry to be pastor at Princes Street. His coming to the School illustrates the overruling hand of God in the life of the believer. Ken Peel had been converted while in the army and afterwards was greatly helped by Gerald McClelland of SASRA, one of the original Barry student group of 1936. The young convert came into contact with Paul Tucker and Omri Jenkins, which eventually led him to Barry. [9]

Mr Fidler must have been glad of the continuing relationship with France. He kept in touch with Pastor Du Barry until his death in 1972, but as for students it was not until 1953 that Marc Nougier arrived from France, followed in 1954 by Bozena Casarovas from Yugoslavia.[10] The two were married and left for the Ivory Coast, returning, when they retired, to France, where they settled down in a goat farm, in a secluded spot far removed from the madding crowd. A few of the former students have kept in touch with

the Nougiers, and one student has visited them in
their home in France.[11] Mlle S. Laffond entered the
College in 1954 [the School became known from 1950
as the South Wales Bible College] and returned to
France to work with the Evangelical Baptist Churches in an administrative capacity, Pastor Guy Appere being the chairman at the time.[12]

The overseas students made a valuable contribution to the witness of the gospel in Talbot Green,
Mid Glamorgan. They helped with the children's
meetings, Marc Nougier's violin playing being a
great attraction.[13] They were also involved in the actual building of the chapel. Ted and Mary Dickinson
were convinced that they should build a place of
worship in Talbot Green. They faced many difficulties
in getting land and materials and after two years the
people of the area were referring to 'Ted's Folly'.[14]
Ted himself did not believe that he was being foolish
and was assured in his heart that the work would be
completed. Local businessmen and craftsmen helped
in different ways, making quicker progress possible.

The College made its distinctive contribution.
Bricks for the building were obtained from a local
person who had dismantled the old Brewery in
Brynsadler nearby. They were carried to the site in a
lorry driven by Mr Dickinson, and Mr Fidler arranged for some of the students to spend their free
half-day on Saturdays at Talbot Green so that they
might clean the bricks, or as the students themselves
would say, convert them.[15] The Dutch students from
the College spent some weeks in a caravan behind
the building in order to help.[16] Maurice Caughey, a
student, helped with the bricklaying at one stage,

and, later, with his father, who came over from Belfast, was responsible for the plastering. Miss Stephens, always ready to help, made her contribution by covering the cost of finishing the front of the chapel. She was also a trustee, the others being Rev. Fred Baggs, Ted Dickinson and the FIEC. The new place of worship was opened on 6 December 1958.[17] Mr Fidler grasped the opportunity to create one of his puns by suggesting that they could have called the place 'Beersheba', since the bricks had come from an old brewery.[18] He presided at the meetings, was responsible for the actual opening and gave the message. A former student, Fred Baggs, related to Ted Dickinson, offered the dedicatory prayer. The College was glad to play its part in this way, and further the witness of the gospel in South Wales. It was a way of taking part in pioneering work, which was always encouraged in the College. It is of interest also that the church still corresponds with a former student in Africa.[19]

Slowly, the interest in overseas mission was renewed. Former students visited the School, including Alwyn Rees (Congo), Margaret Williams (RBMU), and Clifford Evans (Portugal).[20] There was a flow of missionary speakers with some societies sending representatives for the first time, including the Hebrew Christian Testimony to Israel, Ceylon and India General Mission and the Spanish Gospel Mission. Among the speakers were well-known figures like Pastor Schultez and Gladys Aylward.[21]

A few students were drawn to work overseas, and of those who came to Barry during the period 1945 to 1951, one lady left for France, a husband and wife

were accepted by the European Evangelistic Crusade, a husband and wife went to Belgium, another
couple went to Nigeria and another to South Africa.
Stanley and Freda Dawe, from Burnham-on-Crouch,
came to Barry from Heightside, Lancashire, when
the European Christian College was closed.[22] During
their stay Mr Carlos Vansteenburgh (Belgian Gospel
Mission), visited Princes Street Church in Barry, and
through his ministry the Dawes were led to Belgium,
first of all with the European Missionary Fellowship
in the Ardennes, where there was a strong Roman
Catholic opposition. Both did colportage work and
Stanley pastored six people meeting regularly in a
cottage. In 1961 Mr and Mrs Dawe joined the Belgian
Gospel Mission, pastoring three churches and the
husband having a real opportunity to present the
gospel in schools, because the parents could choose
Roman Catholic, Protestant or Moral education for
their children. Both returned to London in 1970, and
after a period of four years moved to Barnstaple to
work with the FIEC, until 1981.[23]

Alan and Betty Huntingford from Walworth (1948-
50), spent nearly twenty years in Zambia and twenty-
one years in South Africa with the South Africa General Mission/Africa Evangelical Fellowship, before
retiring in 1991. They still keep in touch with some of
their fellow students, which is proof of the strong
links that were formed during their Barry days. Like
so many other students Mr and Mrs Huntingford
remember vividly the earnest times of prayer and
they also describe the life of the School as Spartan,
adding that both aspects were a great help for those
preparing to go overseas. The Huntingfords enjoy

friendship with Mr Gerallt Wyn Davies, the present
Chief Executive of the Evangelical Movement of
Wales, and his wife, such friendship bringing together
Barry, the College at Bryntirion and the EMW.[24]

Evangelism

The evangelistic and social aspects of the Christian
message met harmoniously in the person of Major
Alister Smith of the Salvation Army, who was an able
preacher and organizer. The same two aspects are
found in the work of the Christian Association for
Women and Girls, which originated in Mrs Penn-
Lewis' work in Neath, West Glamorgan. She held a
Bible Class for business girls, which led to the formation of a YWCA branch, which Mrs Penn-Lewis regarded as an offshoot of the work in Richmond.
Members were divided into 'Bands', 'Tract Band',
'Cottage Mission Band' and 'Singing Band'.[25] It was
strongly evangelistic but developed the social aspect
as the needs of women and girls were recognized,
and Associations were formed in different parts of
the country. A little later, during the Porth period,
one of the students, who was from Neath, returned
to work in the centre.[26] A branch was established at
Barry, and when it closed as a hostel, provided accommodation for staff and students of the Barry
College. Two of the lady students from Barry went to
work with CAWG, one in Halifax and one in Wat-
ford.[27]

Staff and students were convinced that if evangelistic work was carried on during the period of war, it
had to be continued during peacetime. Laura Rowland

and Miss Turner had already been set apart for that work, Crickhowell being their main centre. The activity was continued at Crickhowell, Brecon and Hay-on-Wye. During 1946 the team had a good welcome in Brecon. The party had intended to stand on what was called the promenade, but found that the site had been taken over by a fair. They decided to visit the manager, who received them most kindly, and arranged for fifteen minutes silence each evening, with the use of the amplifiers. The fair was closed on Sunday and the amplifiers were given for a longer service on that evening. The manager also provided the team with canoes to travel back and fore from the caravan to the open-air services. In these meetings Paul Tucker showed his ability as a speaker, being able to be brief and making use of well-known topics and events.[28] The caravan returned to Barry for repairs estimated at £20. The need was met and by the end of 1948 there was £12 in hand. Soon, there was another need for repairs and when they were completed the caravan ventured out once again. During 1949 the car-evangelist was busy in the Pentyrch area. [29]

Another caravan worked its way northwards and westwards:[30]

12 Feb 1946 It was reported that a site for one of the Caravans had been procured at Llanidloes & it was hoped to start work in July after the Annual Meeting. It was agreed to ask Mr Davies to speak at an Inaugrel [sic] meeting to be held at Llanidloes on July 12th. It was resolved that a Caravan Committee be appointed & further that Revs Davies, R. Rowland & D. C. Rowlands be asked to serve on this.

'Le Roc' caravan, 1948. Victor Duncan (seated) and caravan workers

The work continued in that area, the team moving northwards from Builth and Llanidloes to Newtown and Welshpool. Five students from the Midland Bible College, six from Barry School and three from outside, joined forces, and were greatly encouraged by the help given to them by the vicar of Newtown.[31] During the summer of 1948 the caravan went further west and reached Aberystwyth and Machynlleth.

Early in November 1948 Victor Duncan and R. Towler, the car-evangelists, visited a number of schools and gave encouraging reports of the work at Tal-y-bont, Machynlleth and Towyn. They had managed to reach a number of Sunday-school children through colportage and open-air services. Both workers were due to leave the School in January 1949, Towler being uncertain concerning his future, but Duncan felt constrained to continue with the caravan work. Towler decided to stay, and both he and Duncan were busy witnessing in Barmouth during the summer of 1949. Victor Duncan spent the whole of his life evangelizing. After travelling extensively in Wales he moved to Lincolnshire and visited the towns and villages of that county with a total commitment. He had no elaborate organization, just his caravan, his organ, his tongue, a tract and the power of the Holy Spirit. During the period in Lincolnshire there was one example of three generations coming to a saving knowledge of Christ through Victor Duncan's witness. He died at the home of Dennis Brooks in Essex, 23 July 1972, the same year in which Ernest Ridout and Fred Barwick died.[32]

As the car-evangelists travelled the country they were glad to know of those Bethanies scattered over mid-Wales, those places where they could rest and be encouraged when tired and discouraged. Mr and Mrs Charles Evans were still at Builth, and one of the ministers in that town was the Rev. D. Brinley Jones, a Baptist and an old Porth student. He had the care of the church at Howey, a place very near the heart of Mr Fidler, who continued to visit the believers there after his retirement from Barry. D. B. Jones, who did not have a happy time in mid-Wales, left and entered the Anglican ministry. Moving north-wards the witnesses could look forward to visiting Frank Price at Abbey Cwm Hir, and Edward Evans in Upper Caerau, Llanidloes, both of them former Barry students, and faithful preachers of the gospel in a very needy area.[33] Charles, Frank's brother, had been to the Porth Institute, and ministered in his home county, while Howard, another brother, preached regularly. Both of the Barry students had only brief full-time ministries, but in the providence of God were led to their home districts to bear witness to the gospel in Jerusalem. One service which a Bible col-lege can render to the churches is to provide them with preachers, who are not full-time, but able to fill a particular role, while at the same time tentmaking.

The caravan witness did not take place in a vac-uum, but in an area where there were a number of evangelical centres and activities with which the stu-dents were happy to associate. Local believers and pastors had an opportunity to spend time together at the annual Llandrindod Convention. This was a meeting across denominational boundaries, rejoicing in the motto, 'All one in Christ Jesus'. C. O. Price, the former Porth student, would be there, Clifford

Evans, Franksbridge, a former Barry student, and the
Rev. John Jones, Erwood, who was converted after
beginning his ministry at that place. He became a
prominent figure in the Convention, and after leaving his church to join the London City Mission,
would bring his caravan to work in the area. These
men, and others, would meet with the Barry contingent, which for a long period included Mr and Mrs
Fidler, Mr T. K. Jenkins, Rev. Glyndwr Davies, Rev. J.
R. Morgan, Rev. F. Legge, who had ministered at
Rock, and Miss Stephens. Brynmor Pierce Jones pays
tribute to Miss Stephens because of her spiritual contribution, as well as her financial support, 'Less is
known about her spiritual contribution to those she
met at the convention but she proved a faithful
friend and helper until she aged'.[34]

The resident ministers in the two former counties
of Radnor and Brecon responded willingly to the call
of evangelism. They formed a 'Christian Witness
Group' comprising of Stanley Jackson (Barry School
and Ackhill), Edgar Lewis (Barry School and Talgarth), Robert Rowland (Barry School and Hay),
joined by W. H. McWhinnie (Hereford), and Garnett
Powell (Kington). Before Stanley Jackson left Ackhill
in 1948 another group had been formed to take the
place of the original one, named the 'Radnorshire
Team'.[35] Stanley Jackson ministered at Ackhill, where
he followed a Porth student, Llywellyn Beechey, and
the link with Barry continued through Graham
Brownsell, Andrew Bowden and Richard Ross.

Two other centres have a prominent place in the
story. Reference has been made to Clifford Evans, the
former Barry student, who ministered at Franksbridge

Baptist Chapel. Before he arrived there, there had been tokens of blessing as a number of people in the area were converted. A few miles to the south was Cregrina Methodist Mission, where the Rev. Kenneth Taylor came to minister. In 1945 he was a pre-collegiate probationer, and with the Methodist minister at Builth supervised twelve small charges.[36] Franksbridge Chapel was responsible for one service a month at Cregrina, and the two congregations knew each other well. One of the families in membership at Franksbridge was that of the Breezes of Pont Rhulan Farm. The children of the farm were attracted to Mr Taylor as he had a winning way with children, and this led the parents to invite the preacher to a meal at their home. This was the beginning of serious discussions concerning the way of salvation, which ultimately led to the conversion of Mrs Breeze and then of Mr Breeze. As a result of their turning to the Lord some of the children also became Christians. During a period of a few years a number of individuals and some families were converted, as the Spirit of God moved powerfully in that area.[37]

Kenneth Taylor's intention was to enter Headingley College, Leeds, but he was very concerned with the modernist teaching which characterized that institution, and refused to enter, although accepted. The decision was not a sudden one. He had been deeply influenced by one of Dr Merson Davies' books, and had met the author to discuss the authority of Scripture and related matters. The influence confirmed Kenneth Taylor's conviction that he had to be faithful to the Word of God. The young probationer shared his anguish with Dr Martyn Lloyd-Jones who put him in touch with Dr Renwick in Edinburgh.[38] As a result of this contact, Kenneth Taylor went to the Free Church College, but returned to Wales to minister at Ackhill Baptist Church for just over three years. He was recommended because someone remembered Mr Taylor's preaching during 1945-46.

The link was not lost. In 1957 Llywellyn Breeze, the son of Pant Rhulan Farm entered Barry Bible College, and staff and students, including Ken Peel on his motor bike, would visit the farm. Immediately after his retirement, Mr Fidler visited the home and the area, and Ted Breeze would arrange meetings for him in a number of places. Forty years later Ted Breeze was listening to Douglas McMillan, Edinburgh, preaching in the Heath Church, Cardiff, who acknowledged his debt to a faithful servant of God, the Rev. Kenneth Taylor, the very person who had been the instrument, under God, to bring Mr Breeze to the Saviour.[39] What an encouragement for the servants of the Lord to persevere, knowing that he is sovereign in providence and grace.

God's sovereignty is a constant comfort in times of uncertainty. This was the experience of Mr Fidler and his helpers during 1949 to 1951. However, while rejoicing at the spread of the gospel, there was a shadow over the School as far as the future was concerned.

Cause for concern

What then was the cause for concern? This is expressed clearly in the report for 1949:[40]

Report on the School. It was reported that no further applications had been received & that as far as present appeared only 4 students would be in residence at the re-opening after the summer vacation. It was decided to postpone discussion until a later date. Mr Fidler remarked that the difficulty with regard to Government grant not being available was certainly one of the reasons for lack of applications. The increase in the number of Bible Schools was also mentioned.

It was rather a strange decision to postpone because the situation was serious. One step taken was to write to a number of Christian papers giving information concerning the School.[41] Also the matter of the name of the institution was brought up, which led to discussions and a definite proposal: [42]

In further discussion it was suggested that the term 'School' placed the work at a disadvantage in comparison with other similar institutions. After some consideration it was resolved unanimously that the name be changed to the South Wales Bible Institute. Regarding the work it was suggested that the course should be 3 years except in exceptional cases where by arrangement with the Principal it might be reduced to 2 years. It was suggested also that students might be prepared for the London University Certificate of Proficiency in Religious Knowledge. Mr Fidler suggested he might enquire re this. This was agreed. The possibility of holding night classes was discussed but the matter was left for the present.

There wasn't much enthusiasm for the London Certificate, and the discussion was not taken up, but the changing of the name of the School was taken seriously. The members were unhappy with 'School', and warmed to the suggestion of 'Institute', which would link them with the former Porth and the present Chicago, but after further consideration it was felt that 'College' would be a better term. Consequently, on 24 November 1950, the Council agreed on The South Wales Bible College, 'adding as long as necessary the words "formerly known as the Barry School of Evangelism".'[43]

The Council did take the financial situation seriously, as is evident from one of its meetings:[44]

Financial Report. Mr Fidler gave a financial report. Arising from discussion on expenditure it was resolved that the Council was concerned with the state of the finances & that Mr Reid be asked if he were willing to revert to his former offer of passing his preaching fees to the School & the matter be considered further in the light of the readjustment.

There is no record of Mr Reid's response. The situation did not improve for a number of years, and the end of the academic year would come with around fifteen to twenty pounds in hand, although Mr Fidler was quite optimistic, believing that God would provide. There was a slight improvement in 1954 when a substantial gift was received from Scotland, half of which had to be donated to the Bible House. The Council decided to present the accounts showing the Capital Account separately, and decided also to present the financial need to the students so that they might pray intelligently for the College. Once again the faith of the staff and the students was being tried, but they sincerely believed that the God of providence was still with them and that he would supply all their needs according to the riches of his grace in the Lord Jesus Christ. It was not the first time that Mr Fidler had known such a testing, and he knew what it was to cast his burden upon the Lord. It was also a great help to have encouraging words from the friends of the College, urging him to continue with the work. Trusting in God and taking note of the advice of his friends, Mr Fidler persevered, and generations of students are grateful to him for doing so.

More uncertainty was created, however, when the Rev. J. W. Owen moved from Cardiff in 1950. He had been chairman of the Council, and had just been appointed President of the College. He was the type of person that was needed at the time. In paying tribute to him Council members described Mr Owen as 'the ideal Chairman with the ability to hold together & avoiding all unpleasantness'.[45] Next year Mr Read resigned, which meant losing a lecturer and two persons from the Council, as Mrs Read was a member as well. They left for the Slavic Bible School at Walthamstow.

Efforts were made immediately to replace the lost workers, and also to find extra staff. Mr T. L. Loveridge took over as chairman, after Miss Stephens had held the fort for a few meetings. The responsibility for Practical Evangelism was given to the Rev. Omri Jenkins, who was later to make a significant contribution to EMF, as Home Director, and to overseas missionary work in general. Mrs Paul Tucker was called upon to help with teaching English Language and Literature. Other changes took place in 1954, when Mr Copleston left; W. H. Hughes took over the teaching of Church History, while Rev. Paul Tucker, former student and Council member, started lecturing on Homiletics. During the coming years he was to make a distinctive contribution to the life of the College in a number of different capacities.

There was no end to staff changes during these

years, which must have been very unsettling for the
College. The Rev. W. H. Hughes left Penarth to minister in Exeter, but before leaving suggested that the
Rev. Glyn Prosser of Cardiff should take his place,
and the Council was more than happy to have Mr.
Prosser on the staff. In the same year of 1954 the Rev.
J. R. Morgan was welcomed to the Council and as a
member of staff. Mr Morgan was glad to respond
positively, because of his concern for ministerial
training, his friendship with Mr Fidler and his association with the Porth Institute. In twelve months
time Mr and Mrs Tucker were preparing to leave,
which meant that Mr Fidler had to take the English
lessons and Mr Prosser the Homiletics class. He left
in 1956 to be replaced by the Rev. Crispus Jones, Ely,
Cardiff. More help was forthcoming when the Rev.
Ken Peel, Princes Street, Barry, accepted the responsibility of teaching Practical Evangelism, and Mr
Copleston returned for a period of roughly two years
to help with the teaching. [46]

In spite of the low numbers, especially during
1949 to 1951, and staff changes over a period of five
to six years, the work continued. Indeed the work of
evangelism was extended, as is evident from the
sketch of the witness in mid-Wales. Not only did the
gospel reach that part of Wales, it was taken further
afield, even to Anglesey, and much enthusiasm was
shown by the evangelists.

Wales for Christ

The work in mid-Wales had been going on since
1941, and, occasionally, the students had ventured
beyond that region, but they felt that a more systematic

coverage of North Wales was needed. During the period from 1949 to 1950, Victor Duncan was active in North Wales and had sold £70 worth of Bibles and Christian literature.[47] The Rev. Glyndwr Davies visited him at Betws-y-coed, 'and gave a splendid report of the work'.[48] Such was the enthusiasm that the Council decided to buy another caravan, authorizing Mr Davies and Mr Rowland to make enquiries. There was no immediate success, but after some months of searching the Principal shared some good news with the Council in May 1951:[49]

It was reported by the Principal that in a wonderful way the Lord had enabled us to purchase a new Caravan for Gospel Work: Mr Morris, the Army Scripture Reader stationed at St Athan, having been provided with living quarters in the Camp had his new Caravan for disposal and was happy to let us have it at the very low price of £250. The council adjourned to see the Caravan, and after the Chairman had led in prayer in the Caravan—the Council returned to Committee.

The new caravan was baptized 'Living Waters'.

Mr Duncan persevered in North Wales and crossed to Anglesey during 1952 to witness at Llannerch-y-medd and Newborough.[50] Evangelists were also found for Living Waters, as Edith Young had finished her course in the College and had married Ben Illingsworth. Both of them were from Birmingham, with a Pentecostal background, and were anxious to have an opening for evangelism. They joined the caravan, starting at Neath, moving westwards to Haverfordwest in the former county of Pembroke. Their labours were fruitful and several conversions were reported by September 1953.[51] There were encouragements in terms of small donations, which made it possible to

Caravan, 1956. *Extreme left*: Jim Webber. *Centre*: Mr & Mrs Fidler. *Extreme right*: V. Duncan, Ken Peel.

send an extra £10 each to the evangelists. A larger sum was received in conformity with the Trust Deed of the Porth Institute, reminding the Council once again of the continuing witness of the gospel from Porth to Barry and throughout Wales.[52]

Mr and Mrs Illingsworth concentrated on South West Wales, and had permission to reopen Capel-y-cwm, Solva, which had been closed for eleven years. They worked hard to clean it out, ready for the Easter Convention they had arranged. Everything was ready in good time and Mr Fidler came down to preach, helped by one of the lady students, who sang in the main meetings and spoke at an united meeting for women. The chapel was placed at the disposal of Mr and Mrs Ellison for one year, and although the College could not support them financially, it made a commitment to pray regularly for the couple. Mr Ellison was anxious to be ordained and asked the College to help him, but he was told to wait until the end of the twelvemonth period at Solva. Even then the College could not fulfill his desire because it was not an ordaining body. Meanwhile, Mr and Mrs Illingsworth moved to Mathry, where again their ministry was fruitful.[53]

Mr and Mrs Illingsworth were expecting their second child, and it would not be right for them to remain in the caravan. A cottage was found for them, and the need for a car-evangelist was presented to the College prayer meeting. The one who made the need known was Ted Butts, and he himself was moved to respond to the call to take the gospel to South West Wales. He travelled down to Clarberston Road, where he was met by the Illingsworths, and, almost immediately, moved the caravan to Cardigan town. On his first Sunday there he attended the English Baptist church, but he did not feel welcomed, and was advised to go to the Mission Hall, which he did the following Sunday. They were without a preacher and asked Ted Butts to take the pulpit, which he did on that occasion and for the next six months. The mainstay of the cause was Mrs George, a strong character, unashamed of the gospel. She welcomed the evangelist to her home, and as she had a car would take him occasionally to some of the surrounding districts, where Ted Butts could concentrate on personal work. It was a lonely experience to travel the country, and stand outside the cinema to preach the gospel, but he was glad of the opportunity to witness to the Saviour.[54] There were vast areas without any witness to the gospel.

Ted Butts returned to the College in 1955, and Mr Illingsworth continued with the caravan witness, but in a year's time Ted Butts rejoined the mission in West Wales.[55] Consequently the Illingsworths stayed in the cottage, and Ted Butts in the caravan, with the understanding that students would join him whenever possible. It was difficult for Mr and Mrs Illingsworth to continue, because of the increase in the family and financial pressure. They also wanted to be more independent of the College, but agreed to continue for the time being. Ted Butts made suggestions, not specified in the Minutes of the Council, how to expand the work, but the Council could not respond to them, and advised the evangelist to make enquiries about other agencies who would, perhaps, be able to realize his aims for itinerary work.[56] In correspondence with Mr Illingsworth, the Council arranged to sell Living Waters, and decided to buy a new caravan. They found one valued at £500, but managed to have it for £120. It was made clear to Mr Illingsworth that it had to be used for itinerary work and that the family should live in the cottage. The couple were becoming more and more unsettled, and in spite of receiving help from one of the students, Ronald Price, decided to leave the caravan work. They found an opening for the same kind of work in Suffolk.[57] When they left, the caravan work came to an end in that part of Wales.

The College Council thought that there was a need to restate the nature and aims of caravan work, and did so at their meeting in May 1957:[58]

OUTLINE OF AIMS of CARAVAN WORK which were accepted by the Council

1. To reach with the Gospel the unreached and the badly reached people of the small towns, villages and hamlets of Wales.
2. To work in harmony with sound evangelical Churches and Missions.
3. To gather groups of converts into fellowships, the forming of churches, if necessary, when no evangelical churches exist.
4. To train our own students in this important work.
5. To move from an area as soon as any work is established.
6. Workers to train workers.
7. Methods
     House to house visitations
     Meetings where possible
     Children's meetings to meet parents.

The fire of the gospel was still burning in the hearts

of Council members, and they were convinced that they had to think of the work of evangelism in a church context. When men, women and children were converted they should not be left without teaching, and wherever possible a church should be formed. There was, also, a sincere desire for unity with like-minded individuals, movements and churches. It is a pity that a greater degree of unity was not achieved in Wales during these years. There were different movements evangelizing the country, and more unity would have helped to relieve some of the problems we are facing today.

In spite of the Council's efforts to enthuse the evangelists and give more detailed guidance to them, the response from the students was disappointing. Numbers in the College itself were falling, and of those present very few of them joined the caravan. Clifford Evans spent a brief period as caravan evangelist, followed by Mr and Mrs Biddulph, all three being former students. The new caravan, 'Good News', was stationed for a while at Llandrindod, where the Rev. J. C. Jones, Superintendent of the Christian Conference Centre, kept an eye on it. Mr Duncan did return for a short while, one caravan was sold and another was used by the Rev. John Bird for village evangelism in England.[59]

The Bible House continued to attract visitors and was still a platform for evangelism. Trade was quiet from about 1949 until about 1953, but improved slowly, and students visited the ships once again, taking Scriptures in English, French and Portuguese, and Bibles to the Sully Hospital.[60] Mrs Fidler presented her report in 1955 with 'some enthusiasm':[61]

Mrs Fidler reported with some enthusiasm that the position in the Bible House had improved wonderfully. The arrival of Miss Jones recovering from an operation and having nowhere to live, together with her sister on furlough from Chile, had been Providential. Miss Jones has been re-organising the Bible House, and helping continually at a difficult time of the year. Furthermore, some of the students had caught something of the vision, and were undertaking colportage work. Mr & Mrs Boorne, for example, had paid several visits to the market at Brynmawr.

In six months time it was possible to send money from the profits of the Bible House to the caravan workers.[62]

Life and belief

The number of students at the College was never high. At the end of the war in 1945, 9 students were present, which increased to 14 in 1947. The number decreased to 4, and to 2 during one term, but picked up again with 19 students in 1954 and 14 in 1956.[63] Apart from the overseas students, all the home countries were represented, although there was only one person from Scotland. The vast majority of the home students came from England, a good number from Wales, and a small contingent from Northern Ireland, the fruit of the Rev. Ian Paisley's link with Barry.[64] One of them married and settled in Wales, and another one also married a Welshman and both went to work with the CSSM. Fees, per term, were very reasonable, £15 in 1945, with no increase until 1950, when they were raised to £17.10s.0d. The next increase was in 1956 when they were set at £24.[65]

Occasionally, substantial sums were received by

the College, which gladdened the hearts of Council members, staff and students. At the beginning of the day, 7 June 1951, there was £10 in the Bank, with a demand for bills amounting to £51. That same day a student paid for his fees, and the second post brought a gift of £50, which was quite a substantial gift forty years ago.[66] Although the Porth Bible Institute had been closed for over fifteen years, it took some time to settle its affairs, and when that did happen the Barry College benefited financially. As a result of receiving this money some decisions were made:[67]

The following expenditures were also approved by the Council —£42 for new chairs for the Lecture Hall—£50 for the funds of the Bible House which often supplies Bibles free to the patients in the Hospital, and sometimes to sailors on the ships—£100 to the Principal and his wife who have like all the other members of the Tutorial staff worked in an honorary capacity.

The Council also decided to form a committee, comprising of Miss Stephens, Glyndwr Davies, W. H. Hughes and the Principal, to look into the need for repairs and decorating.

Some significant changes had taken place during the period of just over twenty years since 1936, but, like the poor, some aspects were still present, and had not changed at all. The Rev. Jim Webber, Lôn-las, Neath, a former student, and now a Council member, recalls the special privilege given to him: 'One afternoon a week we did practical work either indoors or in the garden. In addition my special duty was to light the fire in the Aga stove in the kitchen every morning at about 6.15 a.m. and make sure it didn't go out before lunch. Sometimes it did, and I had to relight so we could eat a cooked meal.'[68] Like other former students, Jim Webber used the term 'Spartan' in describing the College. There was very little heating, no wall-to-wall carpeting, bare boards in the bedroom and a little rug at the bedside.

Every aspect of the life of the College was surveyed by the eagle eyes of Mr and Mrs Fidler. All the regulations were applied with the rigidity of the Medes and the Persians. Permission had to be obtained in order to use candles, oil or spirit lamps, and lights had to be out not later than 10 o'clock. Students using gas, and later electricity, for private use, had to keep a strict account of the hours of consumption and enter it on a sheet at the end of the term. All the students had to be punctual at meals, tidily dressed and ready to give an account of themselves if they were late. Not only were students, lecture room, bedrooms and kitchen under the surveillance of Mr and Mrs Fidler but mops, umbrellas, boots and shoes as well. It was clearly stated that 'Men's boots and shoes should be kept downstairs in the boot rack, and not in the bedroom, except one best pair, if desired, which may be kept in the wardrobe. No boots or shoes may be left on the bedroom floor whether under the bed or not.'[69]

These severe aspects found in the College must not hide the more important characteristics of its life. Students and staff formed a family and enjoyed close fellowship together. Sharing, spiritually and materially, was essential for the welfare of the College. Mr Fidler encouraged it and promoted it as he was a

most approachable person. Every aspect of discipline
was regarded as being useful for consecration, to
help students to be more and more committed to the
Lord Jesus Christ. The Principal was convinced that
no effective work would be accomplished without
devotion to the Saviour. It was love for him that
would issue in obedience. Mr Fidler taught the students to look to themselves, to Christ and to the outside world. He would not miss an opportunity to
share concerning the Revival of 1904, and present the
need for a similar visitation of God in the power of
the Holy Spirit. Meanwhile the gospel had to be pro-
claimed, trusting that God would meet with them
and make known his saving power. The emphasis is
found even in the regulations of the College. Most
students preached on Sundays: 'Students not engaged in any preaching engagement are expected to
be at the disposal of the Direction for work in Hospitals, Docks and other Evangelistic work.'[70]

What about the teaching of the College? It is difficult to have a complete picture because there was so
much coming and going as far as the staff was concerned. It is possible, however, to know something of
the doctrine of three of them, Mr Fidler, Glyndwr
Davies and F. Copleston, who were a part of the College for a considerable period of time. Theologically,
B. S. Fidler did not like a slick use of labels, and
would emphasize what are the essentials of the faith:
the inspiration of Scripture, the Trinity, the atoning
death of Christ, the Second Coming, the new birth
and the absolute necessity for holiness in the life of
the believer. He could be regarded as a moderate
Calvinist. His forte was expounding the word of

God devotionally, and the students looked forward
to his taking of the Psalms in morning worship. The
same devotional spirit characterized his lectures. His
aim was to present the content of the books of the
Bible, and he would cover them all by the end of the
course. He was convinced that whatever else the students needed they needed a thorough knowledge of
the Scriptures. A particular phrase could be like a
scent to a hunting hound, and the lecturer would
pursue it for a while, as he did with 'former times',
'the world to come' and the word 'Then' in the sentence, 'Then the glory of the Lord appeared'. Mr Fidler was reluctant to over-systematize theology, and
was afraid of the academic approach to Christian
truth, which made it a mental excercise, far removed
from the needs of men and women.

Adopting such an approach Mr Fidler could dismiss problems too easily. What about the source behind Matthew's Gospel?, 'The problem of the source
of Matthew's Gospel so learnedly discussed by the
critics does not exist.'[71] Yet, on the other hand, being
an able linguist, he would dig into a word in the
original until he would find the gold, and would
compare and contrast what different commentators
would say on a particular matter. He could accept
the suggestion that Peter was an important source
for Mark in writing his Gospel, because there was
some internal evidence for the view, and the external
evidence, the Principal believed, was very strong.
The lecturer's method was to prepare a summary for
each lecture and elaborate in class, being most effective when he was applying truth in a practical way.
In the majority of cases his plan for introducing the

books of the Bible and summarizing their content is
original, but he could, at times, depend heavily on
others, depending on Graham Scroggie's study of
John's Gospel, and on R. B. Jones in expounding
Romans, chapters five to eight.

In the Romans study the Principal did not hide
the fact that he was making such extensive use of
R. B. Jones' lectures. Mr Fidler could follow the Porth
Principal word by word, summarize his points, vary
them slightly and also add material of his own. R. B.
Jones deals with the question asked in Romans chap-
ter 6, verse 1, and suggests that Paul has four answers: '(1). You cannot (verses 1-11); (2) You need not
(verses 12-14); (3) You must not (verses 15-19); (4)
You *had better not* (20-23).' B. S. Fidler suggests that
chapter six, 'may be summarized thus: CONTINUE
IN SIN? 1. You CAN not. 1-11. 2. You NEED NOT. 3.
You MUST not. 15-19. 4. You DARE not. 20-23.'[72] In
sketching the contents of chapter seven of Romans,
Mr Fidler summarized the points presented by R. B.
Jones. It must be added that there are large sections
in Mr Fidler's lectures not found in the work of R. B.
Jones, but it is possible, of course, that the Barry
Principal had a fuller text of the Porth lectures than
what is found in the published work.

Both principals agreed that chapters six and seven
of Romans refer to the experience of the believer, but
developed what they saw as most significant, that is,
the victory over sin. The justified sinner must be led
on to greater things. As far as the 'old man' is concerned he was crucified at the cross, but the believer
has to consider 'sin' and 'sins'. The latter can be dealt
with by the continuing forgiveness of a gracious God,

but sin, in terms of its power, can be dealt with once and for all. The believer can be free from the domin- ion of sin, but before such a life can be lived he must 'die to sin' (Romans 6:7,18,22), and the method is 'death', 'The one and only portal into that life which involves freedom from sin's tyranny is—Death'.[73]

The lecturer elaborated on this theme, emphas- izing that what Paul is contemplating is the be- liever's death:[74]

This gives an opportunity for making an important distinc- tion. Deliverance from sin's penalty and guilt was possible only through the death of Another on behalf of us all, but practical deliverance from Sin's thraldom is not possible apart from our own death as well as His. Our Lord's death was a death FOR sins; ours is a death IN sin, and now becomes both possible and obligatory our death TO sin. This death to Sin is the one door to freedom from its clutches. Not by fighting with Sin is Sin overcome, but by dying to it. Dying to Sin we pass into a realm where Sin has no dominion.

Developing the same point, Fidler argued that Paul is referring to an 'act' not a 'state'. He drew attention to the difference between the AV, 'are dead', and the RV, 'hath died' or 'dead'. The believer should not consider a 'state' in the present but an 'act' in the past. The Holy Spirit would have the believer to look back, 'He would that we turn back into the past and enquire whether at any time in our life as believers there has been an ACT which can be truly described as "dying to sin" ', or as he says in the same lecture, 'a definite decision of the will'.[75]

This act of the will should be a conscious experience, not something taken for granted as a result of a mental assent to a particular formula. The believer is

a person who is in union with the risen Saviour, and
is being led by the Holy Spirit. Baptized into Christ
Jesus, the believer has died with Christ, was buried
with him and draws on the life of the conquering
Saviour. The slave is free from his master, sin, and
being free from sin he is free from 'the law', or, following the RV once again, 'from law', that is the
principle of law, verse 14, which is taken as the link
between chapters six and seven, reaching a climax in
chapter eight, verse one. This is in keeping with the
Overcomer teaching championed by Mrs Penn-
Lewis, and Mr Fidler, like R. B. Jones, took part in
the Overcomer Conventions. Their doctrine of sanctification is linked to their doctrine of man, which
was tripartite. Man, according to this view, is body,
soul and spirit. The unsaved man is governed by his
soulish, natural life, but in regeneration the spirit is
quickened and governs the life of the body and the
soul. The quickened believer is indwelt by the Holy
Spirit but should go on to know the fullness of the
Spirit and enter the realm of victorious living.[76]

It would be impossible to choose Mr Fidler's favourite authors as a good number of writers are referred to quite often. General commentaries included
the Cambridge Bible, James Morison's and Govett's
writings on the New Testament. Lectures on the
Gospels include numerous references to P. J. Gloag,
those on Philippians to Lightfoot, and Ruth Paxson
was one of the favourites in dealing with the letter to
the Ephesians, the person who was one of the referees of the College.[77]

Glyndwr Davies, who was responsible for theology,
depended heavily on Strong's *Systematic Theology*,

and made good use of relevant conservative writers, James Orr and Cynddylan Jones in dealing with God and creation, Hengstenberg, Liddon and Christlieb in discussing the Person of Christ.[78] Hengstenberg is well known in some circles, but his fellow German, Christlieb, has been largely forgotten. He was a professor of Pastoral Theology at Bonn, and remained faithfully conservative in the face of bitter opposition. Glyndwr Davies had a fine series on the Person of Christ, developed on the basis of three points from Dorner on the Incarnation, '1. Assumption of human nature by the Logos. 2. A new, direct creation by God. 3. God revealed in the flesh'.[79] This led him on naturally to deal with the 'kenosis' theory. Acknowledging that the RV reading was 'perfectly legitimate', he argued that the AV conveyed the meaning intended, clearly. He also made the point, a legitimate one, that for some kenotists it was not a problem of interpretation but an opportunity to attack the Person of Christ and his authority. On the one hand, it is no surprise that Glyndwr Davies appealed to Dorner, because he was one of the critics of the kenotic theory, and a highly respected theologian. On the other hand there is an element of surprise, because in avoiding the term 'emptying', Dorner spoke of a development of the Logos after being made flesh, which meant a gradual Incarnation, reaching fulness in the death, resurrection and glorification of the Lord Jesus Christ. After discussing the various possibilities, the lecturer expressed his agreement with Anselm, 'The Son of God acted as if He did not possess Divine attributes', which was, really, a way of avoiding the problem.[80]

Other difficulties concerning the Person of Christ were acknowledged. Does not the very idea of Son imply subordination? Glyndwr Davies responds by saying that, 'The subordination of the Son, obviously, is not the result of the Incarnation, it is something eternal'.[81] The Spirit is subordinate to the Son and the Spirit and the Son to the Father, but the three ar equal in terms of Deity. In dealing with Mark 13:32 the lecturer suggested that it was wrong to find the answer in either the Deity or humanity of the Saviour. We should look rather to his obedience in contrast to the disobedience of Adam. He wanted to know what God had forbidden, but Christ obeyed, being willing to know and not to know: 'He has no passion for knowledge as such. Rather his consuming passion is a love for God's will. He is willing to know. He is equally willing not to know'.[82] In comparing and contrasting the different views, Glyndwr Davies would remind the students that there is a 'plerosis', which should never be lost sight of in discussing 'kenosis'. When he presented the doctrine step by step the lecturer was most helpful but sometimes his patience fails him, and he would dismiss a theory at a stroke. Canon Lilley's view of 'inspiration' was not worthy of attention: 'Scripture brands it as modernist balderdash'.[83]

Like Glyndwr Davies, F. S. Copleston was interested in the 'kenosis' theory. Like his colleague, Copleston accepted the AV translation in Philippians 2, 'made himself of no reputation', bringing out the theme of humiliation. The lecturer published some of his work after the Barry days and brings the NIV into the discussion, which he criticizes for using 'nature' ('phusis'), instead of 'form' ('morphe'). This he regarded as confusing because the two words mean two different things. Copleston concentrates on the term 'Son', which, he argues, is used like the title 'Son of Man', in three ways, as having exclusive reference to Deity, uniting both Deity and human Sonship, and, also, with exclusive reference to his human Sonship. It is in the light of these three points that Mark 13:32 is discussed. In this verse, 'Son' refers to his human Sonship, and, therefore, Christ did not know according to his humanity. This verse must be related to others, to Matthew 11:27, where Christ speaks of his divine Sonship, and the following verse, where he relates the divine and human aspects. Consequently, the three aspects are related, and they must always be discussed together.[84]

With different emphases both lecturers were safeguarding the deity of the Lord Jesus Christ in the tradition of the Early Fathers and Thomas Aquinas in the Middle Ages. Both Mr Davies and Mr Copleston were avoiding the problems of relating the deity and humanity of the Saviour, and the latter would be hard pressed to justify the claim that 'Son' in a particular context can signify the humanity of Jesus. One of Mr Copleston's subjects was Non-Christian Religions, and he would insist on that title, because of the uniqueness of the Christian religion, centred on the unique Person of the Lord Jesus Christ. There was, however, room for apologetics, and he regarded this aspect of his work as being most important. During his long life he gained a thorough knowledge of the main religions of the world, and knew how to approach them critically, but with a measure of sympathy.

Mr Copleston was, originally, a moderate Calvinist, but developed into an aggressive Arminian and premillennialist. One of the basic premises of his theology is that God loves everyone, and he does bring out one of the problems in the Calvinistic view. It is stated that God loves all in a general way but that in the context of Christ's death God loves the elect only. He died for his own, that is, for those whom God loves. There is a problem as is evident from the fact that such staunch Calvinists as B. B. Warfield and John Murray disagree on this matter. Not to proclaim God's love for all, is, according to Mr Copleston, 'grossly to libel the character of God'.[85] Eight reasons are given against the limited nature of God's love, including the two that the non-elect cannot be judged for rejecting Christ, and that there is no genuine offer of the gospel. In keeping with this emphasis the claim is made that salvation is of grace, a gift of God, but the response is that of the person himself, which will lead on to regeneration and new life (Ephesians 2:8). In the application of salvation faith leads on to regeneration.

The Barry apologist had some helpful, positive aspects in his approach to theology. Although he was not convincing in his criticism of limited atonement, he did raise the question as to John Calvin's teaching on the matter. According to Copleston, Calvin was not always clear on the doctrine and there are sections in his work which teach an unlimited atonement. This was before Van Buren and R. T. Kendall's writings were available. Calvin's view is still an issue in the theological world. Another aspect of interest is Mr Copleston's unwillingness to accept what was regarded as orthodox regarding the suffering of God. Traditionally, the emphasis was on the impassibility of God, especially after the Council of Chalcedon, 451 AD, but at Barry they were taught that if God is love, there must be suffering in his heart. Usually this suggestion came from liberal circles in keeping with the sentimental emphasis on God's love, but it is interesting that the theme is being taken up now by conservative theologians.

End of an era

By the mid-fifties Mr Fidler was over seventy years of age, which made it difficult for him to cope with all the demands of College work. The number of students fell, seven entered in September 1957, very few entered the following September and only two in 1959. Included amongst the September 1957 students were three from Holland and one of them, Erik Overbeek, stayed on to help at the English Baptist Church in Barry.[86] Mr and Mrs Fidler were the only permanent staff, helped by a few visiting lecturers. When Margaret Downton arrived in 1959 Mrs Fidler's health was ailing, and it was impossible for Mr Fidler to devote as much time as usual to the College. Consequently, much of the food planning and preparation fell on the shoulders of Miss Downton, the only female student. She carried out her duties, helped by the men, who prepared the vegetables, but at no time was she to be found alone with one male student.[87]

Four important events took place during 1960. The Rev. J. R. Morgan and Mrs Fidler died, Mr Fidler retired as Principal and a new Principal and

Vice-Principal were appointed. Mrs Fidler had rendered valuable service in Porth and Barry, and had
been a tremendous help to her husband. She was a
true mother in the College. When J. R. Morgan passed away, only F. S. Copleston and Glyndwr Davies
remained from the Porth period. Mr Morgan's death
was recorded in the Log Book:

31 May 1960 Funeral of the late J R Morgan who was killed in
a road accident. He had served as Secretary and Tutor at the
Bible Institute Porth and then as Tutor at this College.

Student group, 1959–60. *From left to right:* Noel Jenkins, Don Boyes,
Margaret Downton, Tom Edmondson, Douglas de Cordova.

Council members expressed their high regard for Mr
Morgan, mentioning especially his wise counsel. He
loved to stay for the Friday night prayer meeting,
and his own prayerfulness is brought out in the
Council Minutes, 'We always felt he had been in

close touch with the Lord before coming to the Council meetings'.[88]

Mr Fidler's retirement marked the end of an era. He had been connected with Bible teaching for thirty-six years, fully committed to that work. He will be remembered for his long service, faithful teaching, fatherly care of the students, his linguistic ability, his devotional spirit and zeal for evangelism, and, of course, his puns. He was eighty years old when he retired and it would have been for the benefit of the College and himself if he had given way earlier to a younger man, although, to be fair to Mr Fidler, he had suggested retirement a few years earlier. The Principal was also rather laid-back in developing the College, and a greater effort should have been made to enlarge the work. Former students, however, are not slow in singing his praises: 'I find it difficult to find words to describe him'; 'He was a man of one Book'; 'He did not discuss evangelism, he practised it'; 'I loved him'; 'One of his sentences could be a sermon'; and one former student could not respond in words but the tear on his cheek said everything.

Bernard Sheppard Fidler continued to attend Council Meetings for a few years after retirement, moved to Montpellier, Llandrindod, but slowly the scars of old age were evident on his body and mind. He had to spend some time in hospital but found a home with Mr and Mrs Maurice Caughey, Maurice being a former student, at Bedw Bach, Talbot Green, Mid Glamorgan. They took Mr Fidler with them when they left for Bournemouth for a brief period, and returned to Bedw Bach. The burden of looking after Mr Fidler became too much for the Caugheys and he had to be taken to a Nursing Home near Swansea.[89] The end came on 13 November 1970. There is no doubt that he died a hard death, not that he suffered terribly physically, but mentally and spiritually. He experienced savage attacks from the evil one, and believed that God had left him, which led him to deny what he had preached throughout his life. Faith, however, was restored and he witnessed to his salvation before he died. What a comfort to know that even if he had died in doubt he would still be safe in the Saviour's hand, but we are reminded, forcefully, that many a believer has a rough crossing to the peaceful haven.

Mr Fidler was a versatile person, and one of his many gifts was his ability to compose hymns. It is appropriate that one of them is included as a tribute to him, as a means of keeping alive his memory and, also, as a challenge to all who serve the Saviour: [90]

THE NIGHT COMETH (Huddersfield)

O Lord, the nations in their rage
Fume out their wrath against Thy Son,
Against Thy saints a war they wage,
And boast of victory yet unwon;
But soon Thy Christ shall come to reign,
And all the earth rejoice again.

Oh, keep us faithful to Thy word
In days of darkness and distress,
When rumours loud of war are heard,
Thy Name, O Lord, may we confess;
Until our crownéd Lord we see,
Who once was nailed on Calvary's tree.

The world's dark night is drawing on
Its day of grace is nearly spent;
Our time to work will soon be gone;
We're hastening to God's great event;
But when our glorious Lord shall come,
May we have sheaves to garner home.

REFERENCES

1. 'Post War', *Annual Report*, 1944-5.
2. Mr Owen was from Portsmouth; educated at Bala and London Missionary Society School of Medicine. Served with C.I.M from 1904 to 1927; ordained minister Presbyterian Church of Wales in 1912; pastor at Penrhyn Bay, 1928-9 and came to the Heath Church in 1930. Died 1956. Information received from Mr Leighton Hargest, Heath Church, Cardiff.
3. Council Minutes; E. Willie had left for Jamaica to evangelize.
4. Ibid., 27 January 1948, 27April 1948.
5. Ibid., 28 September 1948.
6. Ibid., 21 June 1946, 27 January 1948.
7. *Annual Report*, 1948-9, 1953; Register of Admission; interview Mrs Selway.
8. Pierre Gardiol is in the Register of Admission, but not numbered; went to work with 'Action Biblique', Barcelona.
9. Interview Ken Peel, 19 April 1995.
10. Register of Admissions.
11. Interview Mrs Baggs.
12. *Lieu fraternal*, 7 July 1985.
13. Interview Mrs Baggs.
14. *Ted's Folly*, the Story of Ebenezer Church, Talbot Green (published by the church, 1991).
15. Interview Mrs Baggs.
16. Erik Overbeek, Hendrika Boog and Heinrich Leo Boog, Register of Admissions.
17. *Ted's Folly*, op. cit.
18. Interview Mrs Baggs.
19. *Ted's Folly*, op. cit. The church corresponds with a former Barry student, Mrs Barwick, in Africa.
20. Log Book.
21. Ibid.

22. Letter 27 March 1995.
23. Ibid.
24. Register of Admissions.
25. Mary N. Garrard, *Mrs Jessie Penn-Lewis, A Memoir* (Bournemouth, 1930), 41-6.
26. Edith Lewis: *The King's Champions,* op. cit., 291.
27. Register of Admissions.
28. Log Book; interview Mr and Mrs Russell, Sidmouth, 20 April 1995.
29. Council Minutes, 27 January 1948, 31 March 1949.
30. Ibid.
31. Ibid., 7 October 1947.
32. *Annual Report*, 1971-2.
33. Register of Admissions.
34. Brynmor Pierce Jones, *The Spiritual Heritage of Keswick in Wales* (B. P. Jones, Christian Literature Press, 1989), 70
35. Stanley Jackson, op. cit.
36. Letter Mrs Lee (nee Taylor), Edinburgh, 1 April 1995.
37. Interview Mr Ted Breeze.
38. Mrs Lee's letter, op. cit.
39. Interview Mr Ted Breeze.
40. Council Minutes, 16 June 1949.
41. Ibid., 12 May 1950.
42. Ibid., 9 September 1949.
43. Ibid., 24 November 1950.
44. Ibid., 9 September 1949.
45. Ibid., 31 January 1950.
46. Ibid., 24 November 1950, 6 November 1951, 25 May 1954, 10 May 1955, 24 August 1956; Log Book, 8 January 1951. The Rev. Glyn Prosser left to be a missionary with the B.M.S. in Ceylon.
47. Council Minutes, 12 May 1950.
48. Ibid., 24 November 1950.
49. Ibid., 4 May 1951.
50. Ibid., 22 January 1952, 3 March 1953.
51. Ibid., 24 September 1953.
52. Ibid., 16 March, 25 May 1954.
53. Ibid., 4 May, 28 September 1954.
54. Interview Mr Ted Butts, 4 November 1994.
55. Council Minutes, 10 May 1955.
56. Ibid., 24 August, 18 September 1956.
57. Ibid., 5 March, 19 November 1957, 21 January 1958.
58. Ibid., 21 May 1957.
59. Ibid., 21 January, 6 August 1958, 14 April, 2, 28 July 1959.
60. Ibid., 22 January 1952, 24 September, 8 December 1953.

61. Ibid., 25 October 1955.
62. Ibid., 22 May 1956.
63. Register of Admissions and *Annual Reports* for those particular years.
64. Register of Admissions: from Belfast, Maurice Caughey, Raymond Humphries, Florence Agnew (1953), Meta Telford (1955), who married Ronald Price, Hay-on-Wye, Barry student.
65. Council Minutes, 23 July 1945, 31 January 1950, 13 March 1956.
66. Log Book, 7 June 1951.
67. Council Minutes, 8 July 1954.
68. Letter the Rev. Jim Webber, 3 September 1994.
69. The South Wales Bible College, Rules for Students.
70. Ibid.
71. B. S. Fidler's Lectures on Matthew's Gospel, copies of Maurice Caughey, Talbot Green, and Norman Lloyd, Cheltenham, examined.
72. B. S. Fidler's Lectures on the Letter to the Romans (Norman Lloyd, Cheltenham), and R. B. Jones, *The Gospel for the Believer* (Overcomer, Bournemouth, n.d.).
73. Fidler's Lectures, op. cit.
74. Ibid.
75. Ibid.
76. Ibid.; Noel Gibbard Collection, Bryntirion, Mr Fidler's addresses, e.g., 'The two natures within the Believer', Note Book 1; Address, Ephesians 2: 1-10, Note Book 2; Bible Study, 1 Cor. 3: 1-16, Acts 18: 1-11, Note Book 3.
77. J. B. Lightfoot (1828-89), apart from the commentary, another important work was, *The Apostolic Fathers* (London, 1891), one of the scholarly Cambridge trio, the other two being Westcott and Hort. Robert Govett (1813-1901), theological writer, very interested in eschatology. An Anglican, but could not accept infant baptism, and opened a nondenominational church in Norwich; still in existence. James Morison was, probably, the founder of the Evangelical Union in Scotland, 1843, an advocate of universal atonement. For the three: J. D. Douglas, ed., *The New International Dictionary of the Christian Church* (Paternoster, 1974). P. J. Gloag, works include, *Introduction to the New Testament* (4 vols).
78. Glyndwr Davies' Lectures (Maurice Caughey and Norman Lloyd), Hengstenberg (1802-69), Lutheran scholar; combated rationalism. Liddon H. P. (1829-90), Anglican preacher. Christlieb (1833-89), German preacher and professor of pastoral theology, J. D. Douglas, ed., *Dictionary*, op. cit.
79. Ibid.; Dorner I. A. (1809-84), Lutheran theologian, J. D. Douglas, ed., *Dictionary*, op. cit.

80. Glyndwr Davies' Lectures.

81. Ibid. In the orthodox tradition it is regarded as an 'economic sub-ordination', as related to the incarnation, John Murray, *Collected Writings*, vol. 2 (Banner of Truth, 1977), 139.

82. Ibid.

83. Ibid.

84. F. S. Copleston, *Christ or Mohammed?* (published by the author, 1989), 340-2. In the Preface he states that, 'This book contains the lectures first delivered to the students of the South Wales Bible College, Barry, and later after I had retired from the Christian ministry, to students of Youth with a Mission, in Crawley, Sussex in 1975, and Vejen, Denmark, 1977.' Some of the Barry lectures were also included in Mr Copleston's, *The Witness of the Old Testament to Christ* (1992).

85. *Christ or Mohammed?*, op. cit., 13.

86. Register of Admissions.

87. Letter Margaret Downton, 5 April 1995.

88. Council Minutes, 10 June 1960.

89. Most of the details from Maurice Caughey; help from the Rev. Jim Webber, Mrs M. Selway and Mr Ted Breeze. Later, in 1972, the Library was enlarged and dedicated to the memory of Mr Fidler, 'With thanks to God this Library is in memory of Bernard Sheppard Fidler founder of this College and Principal 1936-60'.

90. Barry School of Evangelism Hymn Book, No. 23. Another example in Noel Gibbard Collection, ETCW, Bryntirion, Note Book 3, p. 275.

5.
The Old and the New
1960-1985

Ringing the changes

The Rev. John Dart acted as Principal during 1960–1.
Although still young he came with a wealth of experience, having been brought up in England and
China, where his parents were missionaries with the
BMS. He was educated at Cambridge, and taught for
a few years before going to the London Bible Col-
lege, where his Old Testament tutor was the Rev.
John Waite. After another brief period of teaching
John Dart started on his work at the Barry Bible College.[1] He was young, energetic, ready to meet this
new challenge, and was well equipped both spiritually and theologically. The choice of visiting lecturers is significant.[2] They were the Rev. Gerald Smith,
BA, Hebrew, Rev. Derek Swann, BA,BD, Christian
Doctrine and the Rev. John Thomas, Pastoral Studies.
All were products of the Welsh Colleges, deeply influenced by the IVF, and involved with the work of
the Evangelical Movement of Wales. John Thomas
was a Calvinistic Methodist, a tradition which was
also represented by the Rev. Emlyn Jones of Neath,
whose visits to the College were warmly appreciated, especially on Quiet Day. The Rev. Glyndwr
Davies represented the old Porth tradition, with
echoes of Keswick.

Student group, 1961–2. *Inset:* Joseph Fevrier who took the photo.

When the Rev. J. C. J. Waite arrived in 1961 it became clear that the appeal to the reformed tradition,
which had been evident during 1960-61, would be
confirmed. After completing his studies at the London Bible College, John Waite stayed on as a lecturer,
which was a most valuable experience for him before
coming to Barry. With his clear, scholarly and spiritual eye he was already reading the signs of the times.
He could see trends in some individuals and colleges, which were, eventually, to lead to what can be
called liberal evangelicalism. The new Principal was
resolved to be fully committed to Scripture as the infallible word of God, to be balanced doctrinally,
without over-emphasizing one particular doctrine.

The College should be evangelical in the full meaning of that term.

The two Johns settled down to their work. There were six students in September 1960, Miss M. Downton and Mr Neil Jenkins from 1959, Miss M. Grundy, Miss C. Cahill, Miss P. Russell, Mr J. Corney, and these were joined by Mr Glyn Denison in the spring of 1961.[3] The first two mentioned left in 1961, when the remaining five were joined by six new students. The Log Book gives the list and, also, includes some other events of importance during those early months:[4]

Eleven students were welcomed at High Tea at 5.30 pm with which the term commenced. The six new students were: Jim Cannon & Margot Cannon, Joe Fevrier, Glenys Hughes, David Knight & Beryl Williams.

Oct. 4th. Recognition and Induction Services of the new Principal, Rev J. C. J. Waite were held in the Tabernacle, Welsh Congregational Church, King's Square. The preacher at both services was Rev. E. F. Kevan the Principal of London Bible college. In the afternoon Mr Lawton Loveridge, Chairman of the College Council, performed the act of Induction and the Induction prayer was pronounced by the Principal Emeritus, Rev. B. S. Fidler, M.R.S.T. Mr Kevan spoke on 'The Characteristics of New Testament Evangelism' using Acts of the Apostles as the basis of his sermon. In the evening he spoke on 'The Presuppositions and Pre-requisites of Evangelism'. The chairman at both services was Rev. Paul Tucker of East London Tabernacle. The occasion was well supportd by Christian friends.[5]

14th Oct. A team from the College led by Rev. J. H. Dart conducted the service in the church on the Colcot Estate - part of the fortnight's evangelistic campaign to inaugurate the opening of the new building.[6]

Nov. 2nd. Quiet Day. Conducted by Rev. R. Emlyn Jones of Neath. Two main sessions in the morning & one in the afternoon on the Biblical doctrine of Providence—most helpful & refreshing.[7]

Eleven new students were accepted for September 1962, and their occupations are given. This information was not always included during this early period, but the list for 1962 is a great help to understand the background of the students: [8]

Miss Rhoda Corfield	Tailoress	Shrewsbury
Miss Norah Corkhill	Librarian	Bebbington, Cheshire
Miss Dorothy Evans	Secretary	Hoylake, Cheshire
Miss Eileen Miller	Nurse	Belfast
Miss Marion Virgo	Secretary	Hove
Mr David Smith	Bank Clerk	Watford
Mr Steven Cakouros	U.S. Marines	New York
Mr Graham Phillips	Departmental Manager	Eastbourne
Mr Neil Richards	Schoolmaster	Bebbington, Cheshire
Mr Hugh Williams	Motor Mechanic	Pontarddulais
Mr Russell Williams	Carpenter and Joiner	Pen-clawdd, Swansea

They had varied backgrounds and only a few of them had pursued a course in higher education, but the others had qualified for their particular callings. Experience in a particular job was a good preparation for ministry at home and abroad. In terms of their place of origin the usual pattern emerges, that is, seven were from England, two from Wales, one from Northern Ireland and one from America.

The government of the College was reviewed and some changes made. At a meeting held in Mr Loveridge's office it was agreed to dissolve the Advisory Council and form an Executive Council consisting of members of the former Council and co-opted members. Former members were: Mr T. Lawton Loveridge (appointed chairman), Rev. B. S. Fidler, Rev. Glyndwr Davies, Miss B. M. Stephens, Rev. D. C. Rowlands, Rev. Crispus Jones, Rev. Ken Peel, and those co-opted: Rev. Paul Tucker and the Rev. Omri Jenkins. The Rev. F. S. Copleston who had been unable to attend the Advisory Council meetings for some time was also invited to be a member, but although he responded positively he did not take his place on the new Council. The Rev. Crispus Jones left Cardiff in 1961, but the Council was strengthened by co-opting Mr Ernest Lloyd, Mr John Capper, Dr K. Barker, Rev. W. H. Parsons, Rev. R. G. Tucker (Paul Tucker's father), and Mr B. M. Williams. [9]

Soon, there were other changes. The Rev. Derek Swann left for Ashford, Middlesex in 1962, and the Rev. Omri Jenkins resigned in 1963. The Council considered the appointment of a third full-time tutor, and, eventually in 1964, invited D. C. C. Watson, who had been a missionary in India, to be the new member of staff. The family situation, disagreement concerning terms of employment and the standard of teaching were some of the reasons why Mr Watson left after a period of two years.[10] Two of the issues which were discussed raised their heads continually in a college context; the nature of the course and what is the meaning of 'living by faith'. Questions were asked, such as, was too much emphasis being laid on the original languages of Scripture, and was the course practical enough? When an appointment is made, like the appointment of a member of staff, there is an expectation that God will provide financially. When such provision is not forthcoming the individual concerned is embarrassed.

Another task which faced the new Executive Council was that of clarifying and revising the Constitution. This was done during 1963 on the basis of a draft constitution drawn up previously. The name of the College was confirmed, emphasizing that no change had taken place in terms of the aims of the College. Clause 5 was worded as follows:[11]

AIMS AND CHARACTER OF THE COLLEGE

The College is interdenominational and open to both men and women. The courses are designed to give a balanced and thorough training for the work of the Gospel whether at home or abroad. In maintaining unswerving loyalty to the Faith, it is the purpose of the College to train students so that they have a firm grasp of the Word of God and preach it with humility and conviction. Though acknowledging the need for a high educational standard, it is not the aim of the College to offer Divinity Courses based upon those of the Universities. The students will be kept abreast of modern theological trends and these will be refuted wherever they conflict with the Word of God. While not discouraging students from obtaining other Academical Qualifications the College does not regard it as its function to prepare students with a view to their obtaining degrees, diplomas or certificates based on the study of liberal text-books. The function of this College is to offer Diplomas consistent with the Statement of Faith. The Council believes that this step will yet be vindicated; for the supreme need of the Church at all times is a Biblical, expository, Holy Spirit authenticated ministry.

The Constitution was detailed with nine main sections. Clause 4 dealt with the 'Statement of Faith', and there was complete agreement on the major doctrines, including Scripture, the atoning death of Christ, the Holy Spirit as agent of regeneration, holiness and the second coming of the Lord Jesus Christ. A reference to the Church was included, stating the need for the Holy Spirit to direct its worship, ministry and administration. One point was discussed at length, and that was the responsibility of the unbeliever in rejecting salvation. After declaring that it is the Holy Spirit who makes the exercise of faith possible, it was stated that, 'Notwithstanding those who fail to repent are fully responsible for their wilful continuance in sin and in unbelief in the Lord Jesus Christ.'[12]

Aspects of the work came to an end during this period. Sales in the Bible House were low and the space was needed for the use of the College. There was an opening for Miss Rowland to work on the literature stall in Pontypridd market, and she went there with the blessing of the College Council, with the Bible House being used as a depot.[13] The students still helped the caravan missioners, but less attention was given to this aspect of evangelism. The caravan at Howey was in such a bad condition that it had to be sold.[14]

There were, however, new developments. Mrs Fidler, with some help, had been so faithful as matron of the College and as a member of the Council. After her death and Mr Fidler's retirement arrangements had to be made to secure domestic staff. Mr and Mrs John Jones met the need for a short period, and in 1962 Mr and Mrs Lord from Thornton Heath Evangelical Church, Surrey, came to the College as domestic staff at a salary of £400 p.a., free food during the College sessions and free accommodation in a flat at the CAWG centre, but at the end of the first year they moved to 215 Holton Road, Barry, which was given

rent free by Miss Stephens.[15] Mr Gunning, another
Thornton Heath member, served the College occasionally by coming down to decorate different parts
of the College. The minister of the church was the
Rev. Harry Waite, the Principal's brother, which further strengthened the link between the church and
the College.

There was a feeling within the student body that
there was a need for more discussion concerning the
life of the College, and that there should be a more
efficient liason between them and the Principal. Neil
Richards prepared a draft constitution for a student
committee, which was accepted, and officers were
appointed: Chairman, David Smith; Men's Representative, Russell Williams; Women's Representative,
Rhoda Corfield; and Secretary, Marion Virgo.[16] In the
very first meeting arrangements were made to hold
open-air services in Barry, while there was deep
division concerning the merit or otherwise of having
a College scarf. One side argued that a College scarf,
costing only £1.8s.6d., would be a means of witness
and would help the public to identify the students
with the College. An added argument was the fact
that the BTI, Glasgow, had a scarf which was recognized and respected by the public. On the other side
the argument was that it could put people off, and
that there was no need for Barry to imitate other colleges. No agreement was reached on the matter. The
students could aspire to higher things and one matter that cropped up a number of times was the nature and frequency of the Homiletics lectures. It was
felt that more detailed attention should be given to
this aspect of the course.[17]

Staff, students and Council members had to adjust to a number of changes during 1960 to 1965, when the college suffered a severe loss in the death of Mr Lawton Loveridge, at his home, 12 Park Place, Penarth. The feelings of the College are expressed in a minute of the Council:[18]

This Council learns with regret of the passing from among us of our esteemed President and valued friend Mr Lawton Loveridge. Whilst rejoicing over his translation to glory we shall miss his gracious influence, and wise counsel and consistent service to the College extended over many years. The memory of the just is blessed. It is the desire of the Executive Council that a 'Lawton Loveridge Bursary Fund' be opened as a memorial to Mr Loveridge and a means of aiding underprivileged students.

The sum of £80 was received in lieu of floral tributes to the memory of Mr Loveridge. He had been chairman of the Council from 1950 until 1963, and President from then on until his death. He was highly respected in the social and business circles of Cardiff, and was a committed worker at Stanwell Road Baptist Church, Penarth. An employee of his relates how he admired Mr Loveridge in inviting the workers to join him in prayer at the beginning of the working day.[19] The lectern in one of the lecture rooms in the present college at Bryntirion, Bridgend, reminds staff and students of the valuable contribution of Mr Loveridge to the life and witness of the Barry Bible College.

Encouragements and perplexities

During 1966 the Council decided to buy 3 Hilary Rise, to build a new lecture room, to appoint John Capper,

Newport, as president and during the same year
Gerald Smith, one of the visiting lecturers, left to
take up a teaching post. The Council also ventured to
appoint a third full-time member of staff, after discussing the matter a number of times before the end
of 1965, and invited the Rev. John Cook to be a tutor
at the College.[20] Mr Cook met with representatives of
the College, and was invited to take morning worship, which led to his positive response to the invitation. He was a Wesleyan Methodist but was greatly
disturbed by what he regarded as apostasy within
that denomination. After prayerful consideration he
decided to resign from the Methodist ministry before
being considered for the work at Barry. This was
providential timing. John Cook's resignation took effect at the end of August 1966 enabling him to start
at the College the following month. His sphere was
the New Testament and the Greek Language. It was a
most valuable asset to have a person with a sound
knowledge of that language side by side with the
Principal with his expertise in Hebrew. The future
teaching of the biblical languages at Barry had been
assured. It is of interest to note that John Cook was in
College at Birmingham with the Rev. Gordon Macdonald of Aberystwyth, who also left the Wesleyan
Methodist denomination and was the first to take
such a step within the Welsh-speaking denominations.

It was a time of unrest, denominationally. Some
evangelical leaders were calling on their people to
come out, while others were advocating fighting
from within. A number of students at the Presbyterian
Theological College at Aberystwyth were unsettled

and seven of them left the College in 1967, two of them, Michael Hayes and Trevor Macey, coming to Barry. During 1966 the evangelical students were troubled with the liberal approach of all the lecturers but one. Serious discussions took place on the burning questions of the day, 'What is a church?', and, 'What fellowship could believers have with those who did not believe the historical Christian gospel?' The students felt that they were not being prepared for the work to which God was calling them, and reflecting on the period Trevor Macey could say, 'Whilst I enjoyed the food and the sports life at Aber it could not be considered training for the Ministry of the Gospel by the widest stretch of the imagination.'[21] He could have no peace of mind and his conscience was deeply pricked when a milkman from the Rhondda urged him to leave, whatever the consequences might be.

Trevor Macey wrote his letter of resignation in February 1967 and was gone within twenty-four hours. He summarizes the reasons for leaving:[22]

Firstly, the Denomination had openly departed from its excellent declaration of faith and had no view of Scripture that gave any hope of a return. Secondly, there was an inability and unwillingness to discipline known liberals and those who refused to teach sound doctrine. Finally, the Denomination was moving further and further away from Biblical principles of ecclesiology and the rise of the Ecumenical movement merely exasperated the situation.

The former Aberystwyth student was amazed at the difference between the two colleges. At Barry he was warmly welcomed and rejoiced at the doctrines of grace taught by men of the highest calibre. The discipline was 'firm' but appreciated after the laxity of Aberystwyth, and the fellowship was 'remarkable'.[23]

Within the College itself efforts were made to confirm the work. During 1968 new names appear as Council members: Peter Gray, Cardiff, and Jim

'The Bendrox', a favourite walk for the students. *In front:* Shirley Richards, Pam Beswick. *Standing from left to right:* Brian Mockford, Maurice Wade, Peter Creswell, Martin Haynes, Graham Davies

McHaffie, a faithful former student. The Rev. W. H. Parsons resigned as a member of the Council because of the difficulty of attending regularly, and the Council decided to revive the Panel of Reference, comprising of W. H. Parsons, Rev. Herbert Carson, Rev. R. E. Morrish and Prof. Finlayson. The 'old hands' were still there on the Council, D. C. Rowlands, Glyndwr Davies, although his lectures were discontinued, and, of course, Miss Stephens. She was untiring in her service to the College, and most liberal in her financial support, providing an annual sum by means of a covenant gift. [24]

In the *Report* for 1968-69 the Principal summarized the events of the year under three headings. He drew attention to the 'Surprising Provision' of God in terms of students, with a total of 37 in the autumn of 1968. Other aspects of God's provision were the financial giving and the domestic help of Mr and Mrs Lord and Mrs Mary Whiting. Not only was there provision but also 'Spiritual Quickening', especially in terms of evangelism and the prayer meeting. God's presence had been most real during periods of bereavement and this is what the Principal had in mind in dealing with 'Strange Providences'. During 1968-9 there were four deaths which left their mark on the College. Pastor Tucker, Paul Tucker's father, a Council member and a faithful friend of the College, passed away, as did John Capper, President of the College. He had chaired the meetings of the annual day in 1968 and the death of this valued worker was awfully sudden.[25]

As the Principal said in his report, 'Still more strange and perplexing was the cutting short of the promising life of Barry Popham'.[26] He was a diligent student with a 'voracious' appetite for the Word of God. He had to undergo a serious heart operation and did not survive that surgery. His funeral service was held in the College Lecture Room when much grace and encouragement were received from the ministry of the Word. The fourth death was that of the Rev. John Thomas, who spent most of his last day of conscious life on earth at the College. A great number of people would join with the Principal in paying tribute to John: 'The Rev. John Thomas was greatly beloved by us as a College. Nine years ago he was invited to assist us on the Tutorial Staff lecturing to the students on Pastoralia. Every term he visited the College to deliver three lectures on alternate weeks in company with the Rev. Emlyn Jones. His wisdom, experience and above all, his godliness, made his instruction invaluable to our students'.[27]

Early in the 1970's a spirit of unrest was felt in the College which developed to be quite serious by 1973. Some of the students believed that the discipline was too harsh, that the letter of the law was being adhered to and that they should have more freedom in arranging their time. The Principal believed that the existing rules were necessary for the smooth running of the College and that there was efficient liason between him and the students. He suspended some of the students until the Council could discuss the situation, but in the meantime the students involved resigned at different times.[28] The other students, and the Council, expressed their allegiance to the Principal and the staff.

In such a situation it was a great loss to the College when John Dart was constrained to accept a call to Tilehurst Baptist Church, Reading. His departure was referred to by the Principal as 'The End of an Era'. In paying tribute to Mr Dart, the Principal summarized the main qualities of the Vice-Principal's character, 'He combines a razor-sharp mind with a very warm and brotherly disposition'.[29] Faithfully supported by his wife Margaret, daughter of the Rev. and Mrs Owen Thomas, both former Porth students,

John Dart had given fourteen years of dedicated service to the College. Although he was leaving the College he continued as a Council member.

Open-air service on beach at Barry. *From left to right:*
John Waite, John Dart

Much blessing was experienced during the summer of 1974, especially in the prayer meetings. This was a clear token that God was overruling and encouraging staff and students to look to the future with confidence. They were assured of the usefulness of the College when seven students left in 1974 representing seven countries, Australia, Holland, Kenya, Nigeria, South Africa, Northern Ireland and England.[30] The Principal could write with renewed zeal during the period 1974 to 1976. One of his reports is included in full as it is a good example of the masterly way in which John Waite could give an account of the previous year in the annual meeting. It is a pleasure to read, and an added reason is that it comes at the end of forty years of work in Barry, Mr Waite himself having by then completed fifteen years as Principal:[31]

PRINCIPAL'S REPORT
(Given at the Annual Meeting on 7th July)

The Annual Meetings this year mark an important milestone in the College's history. It was forty years ago on the 5th May, 1936 that the Rev. B. S. Fidler commenced the College with eight students. This year also marks my fifteenth as Principal. It is therefore surely appropriate to pause and to take stock.

First, there is much cause for thanksgiving to our great and gracious God. We can say with the Apostle Paul when he stood before the Roman Governor, Festus, 'having therefore obtained help of God I (we) continue unto this day' (Acts 26.22). From the beginning until now this has been His work. Had not His hand been upon it, it would not have survived this long. It has weathered a number of crises. The most serious, perhaps, was in 1959 when only two students were accepted. Unbelief might have read this as the end of the story; faith saw it as simply the close of a chapter. It is heartening to observe how such faith has been vindicated. During the first 25 years, 190 students passed through the College, while in the last 15 years 181 students have received training here.

The College has been going long enough for some of the earlier students to have completed their life service on the mission field. Quite a number have been taken to glory; two even sealing their testimony in the Congo with their blood. While others from earlier years are still fulfilling a vigorous and wide ministry like the College Chairman, Rev. Paul Tucker.

The last 15 years have seen 32 go overseas, to Europe,

Asia, Africa and South America. Eight of these are nationals who returned to minister more effectively in their homeland. During this period, 31 men have been led to pastoral responsibilities in Great Britain. It is good to see that the balance between the work of the Gospel at home and overseas has been almost exactly maintained. Many of our former students are serving the Lord in a variety of useful ways too numerous to specify, e.g. ten of them are Pastor's wives.

The College has always been relatively small, but its emphasis is distinctive. We stand firmly for the great principles of the Reformation and glory in the doctrines of grace. Our aim has been to concentrate on the essentials. We have carefully avoided cluttering up the curriculum with studies that do not have direct bearing on the practical needs of the Christian Ministry. We believe in scholarship but not mere academics. We are above all concerned that those who study with us shall be competent to 'rightly handle the word of truth'. Lectures for us are times of worship. God meets with us and God speaks to us. We believe that the College is more needed today than it was forty years ago. How pronounced is the dearth of expository preaching today!

But what about this year? Can there be anything new to say? Isn't one College year very like another? True, many things remain the same. The rising bell from Tuesday to Friday still sounds at 6.20. College Worship still begins at 8.30 and ends a few minutes before 9.0 – except in the summer terms, when leaving students deliver their valedictory addresses and the face of the large clock at the rear of the lecture room is obscured by the mist of reminiscences! Door to door visitation still takes place on Thursday afternoons.

Yet there have been new things this year. Rice has taken the place of potatoes! This phenomenal hot weather has occasioned a departure from the hitherto unbroken custom that lecturers keep their jackets on. The text on the roof facing the railway has been touched up so that its glorious declaration 'Christ died for the ungodly' stands out with new brightness for all to see. The new House Chairman decided to have fire

College group, 1972. *From left to right, front row:* Jeff Allen, John Cook, Emlyn Jones, Hugh D. Morgan, John Dart, John Waite, Lorna Waite, Catherine Macey, Mrs Lord, Mr Lord

drill early Wednesday morning instead of on Saturday to everybody's consternation. Some, it is rumoured, actually thought it was rather unfair to switch the day without warning! These innovations lie on the periphery. At a much deeper level, there are new things to say after 15 years. Seven times in Scripture, believers are spoken of has having a new song. Its jubilant strains will never die away. We have been deeply aware of the Lord's mercies, His compassions have not failed. They have been new every morning. We have a new song to sing of His great faithfulness throughout this year.

We began the College year with 21 students (5 more than last year), one first year student discontinued his studies at the beginning of the summer term. Today 11 students are taking their leave of us, four ladies and seven men. We thank God for every one of them. With great joy we have watched their spiritual progress. We shall find it very hard to part with each of them, such has been the bond of christian love that the Lord has granted us. All are not sure of the Lord's will for them, but most are fairly clear. Three men have been called to pastorates in Wales, and all are confident that the Lord who has led them clearly so far will go before them and appoint them their spheres of service.

This year has been noteworthy for the encouragements that have come through Practical Evangelism. At almost every Friday Prayer Meeting we have been able to pray for particular inidividuals with whom profitable contact has been made. The students have gone out with expectancy and zeal. It has been costly in terms of the time spent, but how great is the need of this town and what a privilege to bear witness to the Gospel of the grace of God in times like these!

This is the second year with only two full-time members of the teaching staff. We are more aware than ever of the debt we owe to our visiting lecturers. We praise God for enabling them to contribute so substantially to the lecture programme of the College. That they are willing to find time for this work amid their pastoral labours is a sure evidence of the Lord's mercy to us. I feel I must pay tribute to my Colleague Rev.

John Cook, who has not spared himself. If ever a man has given himself to the work of the Lord he has. His lecture programme has been increased considerably during the past two years. But these extra demands have taken their toll and we need to consider actively the appointment of a third full-time member of staff. Our income needs to be increased before this can be contemplated.

Indeed, the entire work of the College is made possible by the willing help of so many. The students themselves are so co-operative and responsive. The sense of being a family has been pronounced during the year. The focal point of the family has undoubtedly been the resident family of Mr and Mrs Trevor Macey. Their duties as warden and caterer have never been exactly defined, which is just as well in view of the wide variety of ways in which they contribute to the life and smooth-running of the College. Their two children sometimes inject a flavour of informality to the most formal occasions!

What of the future? The Lord has been pleased to direct us in recent months eight new students for the coming autumn. Seven of these are men, all from Great Britain. At the present time we are entertaining the prospect of further applications. We would value your prayer about this that our numbers may be maintained and increased.

We began by acknowledging that the work of this College is the Lord's. Under His constraint it was formed 40 years ago and by His continual grace it has continued. 'We will praise Him for all that is past and trust Him for all that's to come'.

The *Report* for 1976-7 recorded the moving of Rev. Ken Peel to Winlaton, Newcastle. He had been secretary for nearly twenty years and had rendered invaluable service to the College. Before leaving he was presented with gifts from the Council, staff and students. Another loss was incurred in the death of

the Rev. D. C. Rowlands, 'D.C.' as he was affection-
ately called. He had been a regular attender of Council
meetings and his contributions were much appreciated. New members were gained by the appointment of the Rev. Maurice Wade, a former student,
and the Rev. Hugh D. Morgan. Hope for the future
was rekindled, confirmed by a sermon preached by
Paul Tucker on the prayer of Jabez in 1 Chronicles.
There was a slight increase in the number of students, and the Rev. Noel Gibbard, who had been visiting since 1974, was appointed as a full-time tutor in
1978. This increased the financial burden, which was
made even heavier when central heating was installed. To complicate matters Mrs Macey was not
enjoying the best of health but the ever faithful Mrs
Whiting received help from Mrs Joan Cook.

During such a time it would have been such a
help to have had the counsel of Miss Stephens, but it
was not to be as she was called home, a loss reported
in the *Annual Report* of 1980-1. She was one of the
last links with the School of Evangelism of 1936. A
tribute to her on behalf of the College was included
in the *Report*. The Rev. Ken Peel commented on the
fragrance of her personality, her prayerful and wise
counsel, her world-wide vision and her liberal giving: 'Speaking naturally one wonders whether there
would be a South Wales Bible College but for the
benefactions of Miss Stephens, when those were so
desperately needed.' She, like Mr Fidler, had the gift
of hymn writing, and a fine example is the one dealing with the mystery of God's ways in providence
and in fulfilling all His purposes, which is the basis
for perseverance and hope:[32]

THE HEAVENLY SEED. Tune: 'Praise'.

Not as our thought the thought Divine,
Not as our ways, O Lord are Thine,
Whose paths we dimly trace;
We faintly sight the heavenly plan,
The wonders of Thy love to man,
The glories of Thy grace.

As freely as the freshening rain,
As gently as o'er hill and plain
The winter snow-flakes fall,
So floods the Spirit's quickening power
When dawns at last the waited hour
For him who hears Thy call.

O heavenly Seed! O Living Word!
O Wind of God, whereof is stirred
Life's current deep and cold!
Not vainly sown, not spent for nought,
Nor void returned, till Thou hast wrought
Thy purpose manifold.

We sow in tears, the seed shall spring
To endless joy: in faith we bring
Our feeble all to Thee;
Great Giver of both seed and sheaf,
Grant us to see past joy and grief
The harvest that shall be.

Miss Stephens had sown faithfully, very often in tears, but had also reaped in joy, and many sheaves were harvested because of her witness.

In the midst of changes and the coming and the going, the annual day came round regularly. It was at this meeting that Miss Stephens would give her report as treasurer, but now that contribution would be

greatly missed. For the students it was a sad and
sweet occasion. There was sorrow in leaving and
parting and some would be uncertain concerning
their future, but realising that they, like Abraham,
had to walk by faith and not by sight. There was joy
in completing the course, in having experienced so
much of the goodness of God during the three-year
course and in the fact that they had formed lasting
friendships during that period. It would be possible
to recall many of those meetings when fellowship
was enjoyed and when the word of God was ministered powerfully to those present, but two are chosen
to represent the meetings during this period. In 1976
the Rev. Derek Prime of Charlotte Chapel, Edinburgh,
preached most helpfully from Genesis 21:22-24, taking
as his theme 'The Importance of the Ordinary', while
in the evening, basing his message on Isaiah 49:2, he
explained the kind of people who are used by God to
reach others. The witness should be a polished shaft
in the service of God and can only be prepared for
that work in fellowship with him.[33] In 1977 the
preacher was the Rev. Douglas McMillan, who took
John 1:1 as his text in the afternoon, drawing attention to the 'Eternity', 'Personality' and 'Deity' of the
Word. The evening message was evangelistic, based
on the life of Manasseh, and the preacher dealt with
the 'Rebellious' one who was 'Rebuked', suffered
'Retribution', came to 'Repentance' and experienced
'Restoration'.[34]

Preaching, teaching and translating

References have already been made to the work of
the College outside of Barry, but that aspect demands

a more detailed study. Apart from serving the churches Sunday by Sunday, the students also took part in special services and evangelistic missions. They visited Gorseinon, West Glamorgan; Bethany, Colcot; Barnstaple and Knotty Ash, Liverpool, apart from taking occasional extra meetings in different churches. At Barnstaple the students helped Stanley and Freda Dawe, former students at the College, in visiting and holding services. The report mentioned a number of memorable occasions: visits to an un-married mother, who could not bear being seen going to church, but eventually did so when she was taken secretly in a car; the conversion of an eighty year old brought to the meeting by an eighty year old friend; and a noisy, almost chaotic barbecue. Providentially, in spite of the noise many of the youngsters were deeply affected by the gospel mes-sage. The outreach in Grangetown, Cardiff was of a pioneering nature, where the students, led by an In-dian, ventured to penetrate the homes of Moonies, Rastafarians, Muslims, Hindus and Sikhs. Every Wednesday afternoon, which was a half day in the area, a Bible study was held in the shop owned by a friend of Pushy, the Indian student.

Summer student pastorates provided excellent ex-perience for the students. The places where they were welcomed included Alfred Place, Aberystwyth, Llangeinor, where the pastor, David Carey-Jones, was a former student, and Memorial Hall, Cardiff, one of a group of churches pastored by the Rev. Mark Eirwyn Pearce, who is, with the churches, most supportive of the College. Links with churches led to students being called as assistant pastors as happened in two churches with close links with the College, Malpas Road Evangelical Church, where the Rev. Hugh D. Morgan was the pastor, and Station Road, Treorchy, one of a group of churches under the care of the Rev. Hubert Clement, also supportive of the College. Both Mr Morgan and Mr Clement were visiting lecturers at the College. Another church which invited an assistant pastor was Widcombe, Bath. Such an arrangement was becoming a more regular feature of the life of the College and the churches.

The training at Barry with its world-wide vision challenged the students to venture to many countries. Going to France meant working in a country indifferent to the Protestant faith, but a number of College students responded to the call to go there. Colin Howells, who was in the College 1963-6, and his wife, went out under the auspices of Grace Baptist Mission, spent some time in Nantes, before moving to Thonon in 1971, where they found a meeting place in 3 Boulevard de la Corniche which they had to leave in 1985, but found a new home in 2 Place de Crete, Thonon, when Pastor G. Appere gave the message at the opening service. Ten years later on 3, 4 June 1995 they were able to hold the inauguration service of the new church building, Eglise Protestante Evangélique.[35] At the College the same time as Colin Howells were Tony and Barbara Hynes, and they went out to Célestat, Alsace, with the European Missionary Fellowship. During the early years the work developed as an annexe of the Mulhouse church, becoming independent in 1976, but continuing to have fellowship with Mulhouse. That was the home church of Jacqueline Wiener, another contemporary at the College, and as she had returned there, all the students were able to keep in touch. In 1980 the EMF started a work in south-west France, and in 1988 Tony and Barbara Hynes moved to Carcassonne, leaving the work in Célestat under the care of Philip Dawe, another Barry man and the son of Stanley and Freda Dawe, who were also former students of the College.[36]

Much of the work in France was of a pioneering nature, especially that at Carcassonne. That is also true of the work in Muslim countries. Apart from the opposition workers have to grapple with a different culture, which includes eating habits. Mary Grundy, working in the Middle East, knew that sheep's eyes were considered a delicacy, and had to summon all her wisdom and tact to refuse eating them.[37] Andrew Swanson also left for the Middle East after ministering for ten years at home. When he left, one of his fears was that Satan would attack by causing him to question the uniqueness of the Christian faith, but during his stay he has become more convinced than ever of the finality of the message of Christ.[38] Other countries, in which former students worked, had been influenced by the Christian faith for a long time and a good example is that of Kenya.

The 1975-6 Report reminded the supporters of the College of the Kenyan connection:

It was in 1970 that the Peniel Evangelical Church, Maesteg, whose pastor was Rev Dr. Eryl Davies, felt constrained to finance the Kenya Africa Pastor Project. This involved meeting in full the cost of bringing over a Pastor from the Africa Inland Church to South Wales and the fees for one year of special studies in the College. Two factors have contributed to

the need for such a project: 1. The momentum of the Ecumenical Movement in Africa. Evangelical churches are
under immense pressure and are exposed to subtle influences in this quarter. 2. Evangelical Pastors are unable at
present to secure a theological training in Kenya such as
would enable them to be on equal terms with non-Evangelical
Pastors.

Dr Davies had been challenged to respond by the
visits of the Revs David Richardson and Maurice
Wheately to Maesteg, 'Especially at an AIM half day
conference I arranged in our pub (THE WAY), in
1970'.[39] The church acted swiftly in spite of the fact
that they seceded from the Presbyterian denomination in December 1970, losing their church building
and manse.

Seven pastors were brought over from Kenya, six
during the Barry period and one during the Bryntirion period. Brief references to the six that came to
Barry will recall the debt which the College owes to
Peniel, Maesteg, and the contribution made by the
pastors to the church in Kenya:[40]

Samuel Mbithi, 1971-2

Stayed with Eryl and Magwen at Maesteg. After leaving
Barry, Samuel spent six months at the American Institute of
Holy Land Studies in Jerusalem. Was appointed Principal of
Machakos Bible College. Sadly, he was killed in a road acci-
dent, 30 April 1977.

Joseph Muhota, 1973-4

Joseph was the Overseas Crusades Director of the Eastern
Africa Team. After a long period with the Crusades he started
an indigenous African ministry, encouraging African pastors
and laymen through seminars and special ministry workshops.

He is a respected leader in the Kenyan Christian community. Joseph's wife, Hannah, was able to join him at Barry.

Samson Bett, 1975-6

Samson was brought up in a non-Christian home and was converted under the ministry of an evangelist who visited his school. There was strong opposition to him from the family, but, eventually, father, mother, brothers and sisters were converted. Samson became president of the African Inland Church Missionary Board and was very influential in forming policy. He continually argued for the involvement of local churches in the work of missions at home and abroad. He also encouraged advances in terms of missionary training, 'In his (western) section of AIC, he won the support for his idea to start the training institute for missionaries. A committee was formed to bring the idea into reality.'[41] In 1986, 12 students took the first course at the new college in Eldoret. Differences arose between Samson Bett and some of the leaders and he was voted out of some of his positions of leadership. He pastors a local church and is still active on many local committees.

Josiah Ogalo Agugo, 1977-8

When Josiah returned to his native country he committed himself to church planting and discipleship training. He is the current chairman (1995), of the AIC Western Lake Region, and moved to Port Victoria, on the shores of Lake Victoria, in order to become more directly involved in outreach in Siaya District, where the AIC has very few churches.

Joseph Kilonzo, 1979-80

He was born into a non-Christian family and the father died when Joseph was a baby. Like Josiah, Joseph was converted while at school. He attended a Bible School and ministered for a number of years before coming to Barry. On his return in 1981 Joseph pastored an AIC church in Thika and then returned to Nunguni, his home district. He is chairman of Mukna District Church Council and pastor of a large local congregation.

Moses Kigan, 1981-2

Moses Kigan was born into a non-Christian family and, like Joseph and Josiah, was converted while at school. He was educated at Kapsabet Institute and Moffat College, before becoming a pastor of several churches. Important aspects of the work to which he contributed, after returning, were the development of a training facility for elders at Eldama Ravine and the construction of the Baringo Bible Institute near Kabarnet.

Dr Eryl Davies moved from Maesteg to Bangor, and encouraged the church there to bring over a pastor from Tanzania to receive further training at Barry. Shadrack Mpanilehi arrived in 1976. He had been educated at Katungulu School and Scott College, had taught at Kabangulu and pastored a church at Musoma for one year before coming to Barry. Shadrack had prayed for years for an IVP Bible Commentary and two of the Bangor members gave him a copy without knowing of Shadrack's prayers. On his return he joined the Bible Institute in Mwanza, Tanzania.[42]

A number of the African students were involved in Bible teaching, and others from the College made a significant contribution in that field and in the sphere of Bible translation.[43] During the 1960s three Barry ladies left for Sarawak, Borneo, followed in the early seventies by a male student and his wife. The first to leave was Dorothy Evans in 1966. During the first period of her stay Dorothy worked in a home for the children of missionaries, preparing correspondence courses at the Borneo Evangelical Mission

at Lawas and visiting a number of nurses' groups.
The next period of Dorothy's service was spent in
Kuching, the capital of Sarawak. Her main responsibility was the care of students at the College, visiting
them and holding Bible studies on Sunday in the
Evangelical Church of Borneo ('Sidang Injil Borneo'),
which led to the start of a church in Kuching.[44]

It was in 1972 that Dorothy Evans was led to Bible
work in the context of a Bible College. It was during
the period when the Field Secretary was giving clear
advice on evangelism and church planting. His message had to be presented to the churches including
the English-speaking people. There was a strong
conviction that both aspects, evangelism and church
planting, had to be grounded in Bible teaching.
Dorothy Evans herself relates the story:[45]

In 1972 the Mission saw the need for the small English speaking section of the Bible College to move from Lawas to Miri,
a town situation where English was used more, since there
was a need to train young men to be pastors in the towns as
well as in the interior. So Ken Coleman (an Aussie Anglican
minister) and his family, myself and 7 students drawn from
various tribal backgrounds lived together under the same
roof. Ken and I did the teaching and lectures were held
under the cover of a carport! So I taught there until Peter and
I left in 1978 for him to train at Barry.

The College grew steadily and one of the students
from Dorothy's time, Winston Edip, is the present
Principal.

The next person to leave was Jean Thomas. She
went with the Borneo Evangelical Mission to work
with the Evangelical Church of Borneo (SIB). Her

sphere of labour was the Kayan longhouse communities along the Baran and Rajang rivers. Much work was done in day and Sunday schools with the main emphasis on Scripture knowledge and preparing suitable material for the Sunday classes. From these meetings emerged the future leaders of the various youth groups. God blessed the work in many parts of Sarawak during the seventies, and the blessing spread from the interior to the coast. The Spirit of God worked powerfully in the lives of believers and many people were saved. Jean Thomas experienced this time of refreshing from the presence of the Lord:[46]

The mid 1970s saw God at work in a remarkable way – whole churches were revived. Initially, in the Kayan area, this meant widespread repentance and burning of charms and 'Satan's medicines' which even some christians had in their homes. Many people who had been nominal or second generation Christians up to this point met with Christ in a real way at this time. It resulted in a high level of spiritual interest and activity with a desire to know both the Lord and His word better. As time went on, this genuine outpouring of the Holy Spirit was sometimes accompanied by excesses that were unhealthy. As a result, the church leaders were asking for more and better teaching from the Scriptures, especially on the work of the Holy Spirit.

Steps were taken to meet with this need for teaching.

The first step that was taken was the establishing of more long and short-term Bible schools. Men and women of the Baran who wanted Bible training had to travel long distances and many found the cost too much. A Bible school was set up at Long Lama and Jean Thomas was invited on to the staff to join the national Christians. A short-term training centre was opened at Belaga where Jean Thomas helped the national pastors. Many from Belaga went on to Long Lama until a full-time school was opened at the former place. The other significant aspect was the desire of the people to have the whole of the Bible in their own language. The New Testament in Kayan had been available since 1970, but there was a demand for the Old Testament as well. The Australian missionary who had done the NT translation was asked to co-ordinate the work, and Jean Thomas helped with the translation checking process. During her last years in Sarawak, Jean Thomas was responsible for co-ordinating Youth work throughout Sarawak and Sabah. She was based at Miri Bible College but travelled extensively to hold short courses in a number of colleges and schools.

When Jenny Russell, the third person to go from Barry to Sarawak, arrived, she spent some time in teaching the children of missionaries, but in 1975 she was made responsible for setting up a Sunday school teacher training system within the national church (SIB). In 1981 she left to work with OMF in the Philippines, and remained there until 1990.[47] Dr Ray Forster was the fourth person who went to Sarawak with the OMF. He entered the College in 1971 after being converted in an unusual way. He was a science research student but felt that his life was meaningless and longed for that discovery that would give him satisfaction and purpose. Ray attended the Commonwealth Games in 1970 and noticed the radiant face of a young girl just below him and wanted to know why she was happy. When they conversed together she explained that she was a Christian and

THE OLD AND THE NEW 187

invited Ray to a gospel service. The message was
based on the words, 'I am the way, the truth and the
life, no man cometh unto the Father but by me', and
the Holy Spirit applied them to the heart of Ray
Forster. He became a new creation in Christ and was
given the desire to commit himself to full-time work.
After finishing his course Ray left for Sarawak and
became the Principal of the Miri Bible College. He
had the opportunity of confirming the work which
had just commenced in 1972.[48]

Two of the students were called to Bible teaching
in Zaire. Eric McGowan, and his wife, Anne, who
had been trained at the BTI, arrived in Zaire in 1973
under the auspices of the UFM. For four years Eric
had experience of such different aspects of work as
building an airstrip, a hospital wing and holding
Bible studies. The couple were able to become fluent
in the language of the people and gained a thorough
knowledge of their culture. Eric became more and
more aware of the need for teaching the people. Encouraged by the Church he started to hold seminars
for pastors. These meetings lasted for over a week,
once every month, and between 400-500 pastors
would attend. When the Church moderator/presi-
dent asserted his authority in 1977 and created division in the Church, the meetings came to an end,
which meant that most of the pastors involved were
left without further training. [49]

After a furlough in 1977, Eric McGowan was approached by WEC to be responsible for Bible work
and was seconded to that Society:[50]

WEC approached us with the need to open a Bongala (our
language) Bible School up in North Zaire. Up until then—

College group, 1978–9. *From left to right, front row:* John de la Haye, Hugh D. Morgan, Noel Gibbard, John Cook, John Waite, Lorna Waite, Catherine Macey, Trevor Macey

anyone entering God's work, from the large area, bigger than UK—had to travel about 250 miles SE—spend 1 year learning Swahili, then 2 years Bible in Swahili. Terrible waste of time and effort. So I started and built the Poko Bible School where we served as Director for almost 10 years—produced over 300 pastors and their wives.

The work was handed over to national leadership to be confirmed and provide the churches of a vast forest area with pastors. In God's providence Eric McGowan visited the College in Barry when Ian and Elaine Campbell were there, and the visit confirmed to the couple that Zaire was God's sphere of labour for them. They left for that country in December 1979. Ian, apt to teach, also has a pastor's heart, and his wife is a faithful co-worker. Both have contributed substantially to ministerial training in parts of Zaire, and are still serving the Lord with enthusiasm in that part of the world.

John Ross, another former student, did some work for Theological Education by Extension in Nigeria. He is, now, a visiting lecturer at ETCW, Bridgend. Cecil Siriwardine, who was at the College from 1965 to 1968, became Principal of Colombo Bible College, Sri Lanka, and pastor of Grace Church. The work suffered a serious blow with the trouble between Tamil and Sinhalese, and eventually Cecil had to leave. Bala, his assistant minister, came to the College and is now ministering in New Zealand.[51]

Colleges at home have also benefited from the services of former Barry students. When Leslie McFall from Newtown, Co. Down came to the Bible College he was advised to take Hebrew as well as the compulsory Greek. He was pleasantly surprised with his progress in the Old Testament language, 'I loved the Hebrew so well and realised its value, namely, that there ought to be well-qualified Hebraists in the Lord's Church to challenge the liberal critical use of the Hebrew, that I went on to do a four-year honours course in Semitic Languages (Hebrew, Syriac and Aramaic), at Queen's University, Belfast'.[52] The careful exegesis of Scripture at Barry and sound doctrine applied in a practical way became the basis of Leslie McFall's life-work. Like so many of the former students of this period he also refers to the Friday prayer meeting, 'that had a deep influence on me'. Having such a foundation he later finished a doctoral thesis, lectured at Belfast Bible College and at Romsey Theological College, Cambridge, until its closure in 1995. At present he is engaged in freelance research into biblical studies, and he says that, 'The bottom line of all my research and teaching is to restore faith in God's Word preparatory to restoring faith in the God of the Word'.[53]

When David Smith left the College he ministered for a while at Eden Baptist Church, Cambridge, worked in Nigeria, researched for his doctorate in Scotland, and then settled down as Principal of Northumbria Bible College. He is most appreciative of his alma mater, but did feel that missiology did not have the attention it deserved. He claimed, even then, that it should be an integral part of the course, rather than having occasional lectures and advice from missionaries. David Smith's zeal in applying his conviction has been evident throughout his ministry, especially in his present position. A recent article of his introduces the main lines of his thinking.

He pin-points two aspects of the present situation which must be taken into account, 'In the first place, theological study on a traditional Western model faces a crisis of confidence', and, secondly, 'Christianity has ceased to be a European phenomenon and has become a world faith'.[54] In such a situation, 'missiological objectives' should 'shape the subject areas of divinity courses'. David Smith illustrates the challenge of such an approach to Biblical Studies, Dogmatics and Church History. For example, he asks his students to read Koyamo's book, *Mount Fuji and Mount Sinai*, 'as a modern interpreter of Jeremiah's temple sermon and then to reflect on the continuing danger posed by religious ideologies of various kinds in the modern world'.[55] When the churches and the colleges do their work properly they will have, not a theology of mission, but a missionary theology.

Preaching and teaching in any country cry out for the Scriptures in the native language. The Wycliffe Bible Translators are doing tremendous work in this realm and some of the Barry students have been enabled to add their contribution to this most important discipline of translation. Philip Hewer, who left Barry in 1971, with his wife, Julie, tackled the problem with that Society while working with the Etung people in Ghana. Progress was made but a prolonged period had to be spent on such a passage as 1 Corinthians 9 with its sixteen questions in twelve verses. They also compiled booklets of folk stories, a simple history of Paga and booklets on wildlife and farming. In this way they were able to communicate with the people and win their attention.

Michael and Joan Payne also work with the Wycliffe Translators, but in South Asia. Michael sketches the difficulties he had to face in translating the Bible into a previously unwritten language. He asked some Hindus a question regarding Luke 5:8, 'Why do you think Peter said he was sinful?', and the answer was, 'Because he had killed all those fish'. When asked, on the basis of John 18:8, 'Who was Jesus referring to by "these men"?', the answer was, 'The soldiers who had come to arrest him.' [56] Michael and the other translators had to understand how the mind of the native person was working, as he was being introduced to the completely new world of the Scriptures. It was not just one dialect that had to be considered. The translators had to ask the question, 'Which is the most prestigious dialect in the language?' When that matter was decided would the speakers of other dialects accept the dialect chosen for the translation? And, whatever the merits or demerits of a translation, would the national church accept it? These are some of the challenges to translating the Scriptures for minority ethnic groups. In doing the work the translators in South Asia used all possible reliable versions, always referring back to the Greek original.

Michael Payne gives a summary of the work which has been accomplished until 1995, and at the same times refers to some of the difficulties of working in a foreign country:[57]

How far have we gone in the translation? By God's help we have translated Luke, Acts, some other NT & OT portions and we are half way through John. Though our main focus is on the NT, we also hope to translate some OT books beginning with Genesis. What is it like living here? It's not easy. Being a desert area the climate is hot and dry, with very high summer temperatures. Social custom is against women going out of the house very much. And home schooling is a challenge, both for our teenage daughter who is 8hrs by road from other ex-patriates of her age, and also for her parents.

Much grace is given to Michael and Joan to persevere. It is their prayer that God will raise up nationals to do the work, and that under the blessing of God's Spirit the desert will blossom and rejoice.

Last years at Barry

A reference in the 1981-82 *Report* gives a hint of unrest and the willingness to look for new premises. Staff and Council members were soon on the alert for a suitable place. It was known that the Evangelical Movement of Wales was interested in developing theological education and as there were personal links, in terms of membership of Council and General Committee, a joint effort was a possibility. The Council approached the General Committee of the Movement during 1982, and this led to a number of exploratory meetings, and ultimately to an official agreement to form a new college incorporating the South Wales Bible College. A Working Party was set up to consider details and procedure and in one of its meetings during 1983 it recommended that the new council should consist of the existing Barry Council and an equal number from the Evangelical Movement. The recommendation, and other details, were presented to the Barry Council and the General Committee of the EMW. They were accepted by both parties, but there was a minority within the Movement that disagreed.

An EMW Memorandum, dated 1 July 1983, was discussed by the College Council and the Movement representatives on the Working Party. The membership of the new council was confirmed, and the report and that of a sub-committee to discuss the curriculum were presented to the first official meeting of the new college on 5 December 1983, at Bryntirion, the EMW conference centre at Bridgend, Mid Glamorgan.

In agreement with a minute of the 27 September 1983, the Council was made up of twenty-four members, twelve each from Barry and the EMW. The Barry representatives were: Dr Ken Barker, Messrs Maurice Garton, Ernest Lloyd, Clem Roberts, Revs Jim Cannon, Hugh Morgan, Paul Tucker, Maurice Wade, Derek Swann, John Dart, Jim Webber and another person to take John Waite's place. The EMW representatives were: Revs J. Elwyn Davies, Eryl Davies, Sulwyn Jones, Peter Milsom, Neville Rees, Gwynn Williams, Derek Garwood, Andrew Davies, Gareth Davies, Arthur Pritchard, Bruce Powell and Gwilym Roberts. Working parties were set up to look after finance, the erection of a new building and accommodation. The Rev. Elwyn Davies was appointed President and the Rev. John Waite was invited to be Senior Tutor.

It was a time of heart-searching for the Barry members of staff. They accepted the need for changes but did not feel that all of those discussed had been worked out clearly. They had not been consulted regarding the curriculum and a distinction was made between 'Principal' and 'Senior Tutor'. John Waite became convinced that he would have to leave, trusting that God would open up another sphere of service. The Lord led him to a pastorate in Sheffield, where he and Lorna, his wife, soon settled down. The Revs John Cook and Noel Gibbard agreed to continue as members of staff. Consequently, the Council had to reconsider the staffing of the new College. After discussing three names in turn, it was decided on 19 October 1984 to invite Dr Eryl Davies, Bangor, to be Senior Tutor. He made known his positive response in the Council Meeting of 19 November and in a letter dated 27th of the same month. The Rev. Elwyn Davies met with the three members of staff, leading a helpful discussion on relationships and curriculum possibilities, and preparing the way for the proposed opening of the College in September 1985.[58]

The chairman during this period was the Rev. Paul Tucker, who had held that position since 1963. He continued to chair the Barry College Council meetings until 1985, but expressed his wish that someone else would lead the new Council, and the Rev. Hugh D. Morgan was chosen in 1983. Paul Tucker's relationship with the College must be unique, in that he was a student, lecturer, Council member and chairman, and secretary, besides preaching regularly at the autumn meetings for over twenty years. He was elected a member as far back as 1950, and is still on the Council but finds it difficult to attend regularly because of ill-health.

The story of the period 1960 to 1985 cannot end without a tribute to the Rev. John Waite, who, like

Mr Fidler, had given twenty-four years of faithful service to the College in Barry. The length of service deserves thanks but even more so does its quality. John Waite had gained a thorough knowledge of the original languages of Scripture, and made it a basis of careful exegesis and exposition of the Word of God. As John Waite himself said, commenting on the lack of clarity in preaching, 'There is all too little attention to careful and accurate exegesis and exposition'.[59] The students highly valued his lectures on the prophets and many of them have commented on the way in which he dealt with passages from Isaiah, deep in content and devotional in spirit. They could depend on having detailed information and application from the books of Samuel and Kings, when good commentaries on those sections of Scripture were scarce. The Principal was no mean preacher, and although he would not want the students to imitate him, a great number of them have benefited from his presentation of the gospel, which was expository and applicatory. John Waite and his wife, Lorna, were committed to the witness of the College, and she spent innumerable hours in her cramped office for the sake of the smooth running of the College. Their move to Sheffield has been confirmed by evident tokens of God's blessing.

John Waite was more than ready to pay tribute to other workers in the College. In the early spring of 1985 Trevor and Catherine Macey with their children left for Bude, Cornwall. The Principal thanked them for their twelve years work as warden and caterer, 'We are indebted to them for their selfless service'.[60] Apart from paying tributes, one important event was still to come, and that was the annual day of 1985, held at Bethel, Barry. Emotions were touched but some relief was found in the comment of the leaving students that they had left their mark on the College as it was closing. Amongst the many friends present was the Rev. Derek Garwood, Pont-rhyd-yr-ynn, Gwent, who was a former student, talking merrily to those around him and leaving on his moped. The following morning news was received of his sudden death. He was an enthusiastic supporter of the new venture, and always had helpful suggestions to make on the library committee. Most of his books were donated to the new College library.

A good number remained for the evening meal after the services of the day. Gareth James was the House Chairman and recalls the occasion:[61]

The end of year meal for the students, lecturers and their families was a time of sadness and yet of expectation. We had, as a parent and guest, Professor Boyd from Edinburgh, who closed in prayer, and then we sang, 'How good is the God we adore' - the words appropriate for the work of both colleges.

Gareth could not relax as he was continuing in office until Easter 1986.

REFERENCES

1. Interview John Dart, 15 February 1995.
2. Council Minutes, 28 September 1960.
3. Log Book, 27 September 1960, Register of Admissions for 1960-61.
4. Log Book, 26 September 1961.
5. Ibid.
6. Ibid.
7. Ibid.
8. *Annual Report*, 1962-3.

9. Council Minutes, 17 June 1960, 26 May 1961, 18 May 1962, 9 January, 23 July 1963.

10. Ibid.

11. Ibid., 2 April 1963.

12. Ibid.

13. Ibid., 18 May 1962.

14. Ibid., 1 October 1963, 14 January 1964.

15. Ibid., 18 May, 3 October 1962, 1 October 1963.

16. House Committee Minute Book, 26 April 1963.

17. Ibid., 12 February 1965, 8 February, 19 March 1966.

18. Council Minutes, 22 January 1965; brief obituary, 'Deaths', *South Wales Echo*, 14 January 1965.

19. Information from Mr Colin Rees, Penarth, 15 December 1994.

20. Council Minutes, 10 December 1965, 8, 21 February, 5 April 1966.

21. Letter 8 June 1995. Trevor Macey's pastor at the Heath was at the time fighting from within the denomination, but, eventually, pastor and congregation seceded.

22. Ibid.

23. Ibid.

24. Council Minutes, 1 October 1968.

25. Interesting references and photograph of Mr John Capper, Geraint D. Fielder, *'Excuse me, Mr Davies—Hallelujah!'* (IVP and EPW, 1983), 209-10.

26. *Annual Report*, 1968-9.

27. Ibid.; Council Minutes, 8 July 1969.

28. Council Minutes, 29 February 1972-8 July 1974, List of students in Register of Admissions.

29. *Annual Report*, 1973-4.

30. Ibid.

31. 'The Faithfulness of God', *Annual Report*, 1975-6.

32. Barry School of Evangelism Hymn Book, No. 15.

33. *Annual Report*, 1975-6.

34. Ibid., 1976-7.

35. *Lieu fraternal*, 7 July 1985, Prayer and News Letter, May 1995.

36. Letter from Tony and Barbara Hynes, 21 August 1995.

37. *Annual Report*, 1966-7; *Remembrancer*, 1976.

38. Prayer Letter, April 1995.

39. Information from Dr Davies.

40. Information received from Dr Davies, Mr Leslie James, Maesteg, Dr Dick Anderson, letter 1 June 1995, Rev. Jonathan Hilderbrandt, letter 14 June 1995.

41. Klaus Fiedler, *The Story of Faith Missions* (Regnum Lynx, 1994), 378, 383 n. 46, 47; D. Anderson, *We Felt like Grasshoppers* (Crossway,

1994), 237, 327-8.

42. Information Dr Davies; *Annual Report*, 1976-7.
43. Dates not given for Donald Boyes; left, probably 1959. He worked with the Bolivian Indian Mission, and went out, with his wife, to Brazil in 1962. Mr and Mrs Boyes taught at the Quillacollo Bible Institute preparing Quechua Indians for Christian service.
44. Letter, 17 April 1995.
45. Ibid. Dorothy's husband, Peter Sim, came to Barry to be trained at the Bible College. Both returned to Sarawak for a period; now living in Australia.
46. Letter, 12 June 1995.
47. Letter from Jenny Russell, n.d.
48. Testimony of Ray Forster, *Annual Report*, 1970-1.
49. Letter, 16 May 1995.
50. Ibid.
51. Jonathan Chiniah, also from Sri Lanka, has a ministry in the Rhondda.
52. Letter, 29 June 1995.
53. Ibid.
54. 'A Theology of Mission or a Missionary Theology?', *Scottish Bulletin of Evangelical Theology*, Spring 1995.
55. Ibid.
56. Letter, 29 May 1995.
57. Ibid.
58. Account based on Council Minutes; the most important dates have been included.
59. College Newsletter, 1983.
60. Ibid.
61. Letter, 1 May 1985.

6.
God's Provision at Bryntirion, the 'Pleasant Hill'
1985–

Dr Eryl Davies, the Senior Tutor, had a long established link with the Barry College, which had been formed during his days at Maesteg, Mid Glamorgan, where he ministered from 1959 until 1975. After leaving school at an early age, he prepared himself for higher education, gaining a degree in the arts and theology. He went on to obtain an M.A. (London), and Ph.D. (Wales). From 1975 until 1985 he was the pastor of the Evangelical Church at Bangor, North Wales. For some time he had shown interest in Christian literature, was editor of *Foundations* and author of two booklets, which prepared the way for further publications.[1] He, and his colleagues, John Cook and Noel Gibbard, had to adapt themselves as best as possible to the unfinished building at Bryntirion, but the EMW showed much kindness and relieved the problems considerably. The Rev. Elwyn Davies, as President, was always ready with his advice, and a welcome contribution was made by the visiting lecturers, the Rev. Hugh Morgan, Malpas, Newport and the Rev. Hubert Clement, Tonypandy.

Early days

The House Chairman and some of the students and

staff faced the task of packing the College books and
taking them to Bryntirion. Acting on the belief that
common grace is found in the most unlikely places,
they managed to find the best boxes in the nearby
off-licence in Barry. The whisky boxes were ideal for
the task. They arrived safely, ready for their new
home, but where exactly was that place? The new
building was not completed, but necessity is the
mother of invention, as explained by Gareth James:[2]

A library was finally organized—in one half of the table ten-
nis room. Stud partitioning was erected and plaster board
and a lockable door installed. Shelves? They were easy—2 or
3 bricks either end and a plank across the top. Then 2 or 3
more bricks and another plank. Then rummage through the
boxes of books to find those currently required, then books
for the following term. It was up and running in a week-
end—though with only one copy of each book we had to
learn patience, kindness and sharing.

Gareth was able to help Dr Davies to work out the
role of the students, and, also, to find a vacant corner
to be used as a lecture room.

The new college, officially known as the Evangelical Theological College of Wales (ETCW), Bryntirion,
Bridgend, started with twenty-two students, which
increased during the second term to twenty-six.
They included the ten who had come from Barry:
Gareth James, who went as an assistant to Ponte-
fract, and then moved on to be pastor at Humber-
side; Paul Clement, who spent a period as assistant
at Malpas Road, Newport, before going on to Uck-
field, East Sussex; Tudor Jones, who accepted a call
to the Welsh Congregational Church at Penydarren,
Merthyr Tydfil; Jean Andreller, who, shortly after

leaving, became the pastor of an Estonian Church in Toronto, Canada; Roger Lindie, who married Linda, a former student, was without a pastorate for a brief time after leaving the College, but was eventually called to a church in London; Bert Weenink, who had considered going overseas, permanently, after working in Belgium for a while, returned to Wales and was called to the Baptist Church at Pont-rhyd-yr-ynn, to succeed Derek Garwood, a former student and the one taken so suddenly in 1985. The other students were Sharon Boyd, who did not enjoy the best of health while at the College, but was able to prepare herself for translation work; Billy McCartney who settled near Shrewsbury without a pastorate, but serving the local churches; and Bob Monckton who returned to teaching, also serving the local churches of Barry and district; and Colin Barrett.

It was a great relief for all concerned when the new building was completed. It was possible to relax a little and make more progress as far as the course and the life of the College were concerned. New appointments were made to strengthen both the office and teaching staff. Miss Ann Matthews, in nearby Bridgend, was available for office work before going out in twelve months time to Bolivia with SIM. Her work was much appreciated during this brief period. Ann was replaced by Mrs Chris Connor, Cardiff, and she is still at her post. Not only is she a most efficient secretary, but also a person who is sensitive to all kinds of need in the College, always ready to respond to them. There is no doubt that she has been endowed with a double portion of patience. The College benefited greatly when Mr John Sieczko, Bangor,

North Wales, joined the staff, as he was a Hebrew specialist, but felt called in another direction in 1990.

During the early days at Bryntirion it was decided to implement one of the aspects of the College's policy in a new way. For a long time during the Barry period many of the students had been involved in student pastorates during the summer holidays. There was a strong conviction that the students should be involved in church work at a practical level. The same conviction was expressed at Bryntirion, 'This training will be thoroughly Biblical, academic, spiritual and integrated increasingly into church life in Wales and further afield.'[3] The new development was that of 'placement', which made the practical work an integral part of the College course. A student was invited, or allocated, to a particular church for a period of weeks, during the month of May at the beginning, but later changed to a different time of the year. Of the twenty-one churches that took part in 1986, six were pastorless and this meant an extra demand on the students placed in those places. Response from students and churches expressed appreciation of the arrangement. Churches were glad to have the students, pastors were happy to share with them and the students themselves grasped the opportunity to apply the teaching in the classroom to a church situation.

A most precious aspect of the experience was taking part in varied activities: preaching, listening to preaching, teaching in Sunday school, taking children's services, visiting homes, schools and hospitals. While visiting they had to face most difficult situations, and learn how to speak with the terminally ill

ETCW group photo, 1985–6. *Staff from left to right, front row:*
Ann Matthews (second from left), Noel Gibbard, Eryl Davies, John Cook

and those opposed to the gospel. In many of the schools they witnessed a resentment to Scripture teaching, but openness to discuss matters which the pupils thought were important. A new experience for most of the students was being present at elders/deacons' meetings, where mortar and bricks were discussed, and weighty matters such as the call to the ministry and evangelism.

Placement offers an opportunity for self-assessment and when the students have been honestly engaged in this discipline they have benefited from it. A more recent development is to ask them to keep a diary of their work during placement, and it is expected that some self-criticism will be included in the entries. It is very pleasing to find comments on their own preaching, such as, 'Tackled too difficult a task', 'attempted too much', 'too much content', 'a little more application needed', and 'too long'.[4] These comments, together with those received from the churches, help the students to learn much in the realm of preaching. The ladies are not neglected, although some of them feel that there is not enough active participation for women. The reason for this, in some cases, is the smallness of the church, but in other cases it is the lack of understanding regarding the place of the woman in the Church. A few churches have a recognized lady worker, and she takes care of the visiting student. This is an excellent arrangement.

1987: A significant year

The year 1987 was significant in many ways, as the coming of new workers has already suggested. Even in terms of the weather it is a time to be remembered because the water pipes froze and the first day of the spring term had to be cancelled. Soon after settling down in the College the wives of students expressed a strong desire to have a meeting of their own, and the first one was held during the autumn term of 1987.[5] This meeting is still held and is proving to be a real help for the wives. It gives them a sense of belonging, an opportunity to clarify their particular role in the ministry, helps them to be supportive of their husbands and provides them with good instruction. There are opportunities for worship, teaching, discussion, and, of course, there is time for a coffee break. During that year Council and Staff discussed the possibility of introducing a validated two-year diploma course which would lead on to a third year degree in theology. Before the end of the year attention was given to postgraduate work in conjunction with the Polytechnic of Wales, Pontypridd, and, also, a correspondence course.[6] All these discussions bore fruit in due time and some attention must be given to each one of these developments.

During the early period of discussing the diploma, enquiries had been received concerning the possibilities of research work. The Rev. John Cook was also personally interested and registered for an M.Phil., but did not pursue it. Two of the students expressed interest but because of difficulties in working out the registration procedure with the Polytechnic of Wales there was a long delay before the first registration was recorded. The development renewed the discussion regarding the emphasis on the academic side of the College. Some felt that it was being over-emphasized, while others did not see the need for it, and apart from these reservations there was the practical aspect of coping with the new demand.

Staff and Council agreed that a research programme should be introduced, because if God had given the ability to specialize, it should be used and developed. This did not mean that a chosen subject should be of academic relevance only; it should, rather, be chosen in the light of future possibilities for the researcher, and usefulness to the Church generally or to the Church in a particular area.

The thinking of the College on this matter is clearly presented by Dr David Cook, Oxford, in a lecture delivered at Bryntirion.[7] In the lecture, entitled 'The Purpose of Christian Research', he argued that there were three central factors to be considered. First of all, he dealt with 'The right view of God'. God is the Creator, and if he has created the world it should make sense. He has created and there is order and purpose in his world. God is the ground of all truth, and we should not shun the pursuit of it. Secondly, the lecturer dealt with 'The right view of scholarship'. The Christian researcher has to distinguish between 'truth' and 'validity', because it is possible to have the latter without having the former, but the right way forward is to have both. This involves seeing the positive and the negative aspects in the works of those who disagree with us, and he reminded his hearers in this context, that this is attributed to the fact that man has been created in the image of God. One paragraph should be included in full:[8]

For Christians, the question as to motives for engaging in research should always be borne in mind. Whilst some look for
financial gain, or to ascertain truth for its own sake or to gain
qualification as a means to an end, e.g., to teach at a certain
level, or even ultimately to be of service to others, as the ob-
jective of their research, so it is with believers that they
should want to learn to think as accurately as they can as this
should make them better communicators of the truth and
thus the church should derive benefit from their work.

Research calls for integrity and honesty and the believer sees both aspects in the light of his relationship
to God.

The third aspect with which Dr Cook dealt was,
'The right view of the scholar'. The researcher must
always be grateful for the opportunity afforded to
him, and be conscious at all times of his responsibility to God. Not only is he an individual, he is also
'in community', working within the sphere of the
family, supervisors, the scholastic community, and
the Church. The lecturer dealt briefly with these different aspects. In commenting on the family, he reminded the male-dominated audience that many
researchers achieved their objectives 'by the sweat of
their frau'. Dr Cook made some very practical applications in closing his address. He made helpful suggestions regarding discipline and taking care of the
body as well as the mind. The last point of application was that research is not 'training for the ministry', but it is 'an aspect of ministry'. That is, 'The
process of research should make Christians more
effective as stewards, and as servants, of the Lord
Jesus Christ and his Church.'[9]

Examples of the subjects taken for research will

illustrate the applicatory nature of the work. A member of staff is looking at 'Translation Methodology used in the New Welsh Bible'. His study should be a tremendous help to Welsh-speaking Christians in assessing the translation. Nothing is more important than having a good, dependable version of the Word of God. Hermeneutics, a study of the principles regarding the interpretation of Scripture, is attracting much attention in our day, and an experienced pastor is devoting time to this subject. He is concentrating on 'The Holy Spirit and Biblical Hermeneutics'. A study of Historical Theology should benefit all Christians, especially pastors. It is good to know how leaders in the past have dealt with doctrinal issues. An American pastor, long attracted to Wales, is studying the work of the Welsh Puritan, Vavasor Powell, and his teaching on the application of salvation as related to the articles of the Westminster Assembly. The nature of the Calvinistic doctrinal tradition has received considerable attention in recent years, and it will be good to know where, exactly, Vavasor Powell stood in this tradition.

Serious moral issues have to be faced in our day, and any clear guidance in the light of Scripture is appreciated. One student is tackling a very difficult problem, 'Denominational Interpretation of the Spiritual Status of the Still-born'. We also need clear principles for outreach work, and the work of a researcher on, 'Contemporary Evangelical Church Outreach in a Working-class Area', should make a valuable contribution in this sphere. So many different voices are being heard, and so many experiments taking place, that many Christians are confused. There is dire need in this realm, especially in working-class areas. Developments world-wide are taken into account as well. A former student from Venezuela has made a substantial contribution to our understanding of Liberation Theology. Having the Spanish language, he was able to study original sources, and he has presented useful insights into this movement which has gripped parts of South America and Africa. The findings will enable us to assess the theology and see how it is contrary to the teaching of Scripture.

A former worker with the Red Sea Mission has chosen a fascinating subject, 'Conversion and Baptism for Converts from Islam'. The former missionary is considering the linguistic, theological, psychological and medical viewpoints concerning 'conversion' and 'baptism'. This involves a detailed study of the two terms in the New Testament and Islam. Suggested 'dynamic equivalents' between Christianity and Islam are considered and criticized. The researcher 'is anxious that Missions seek to keep their Muslim outreach methods within a scriptural framework and that modern methods (e.g. business management paradigms and psychological techniques), are not allowed to obtrude to the detriment of Scripture.'

An Indonesian student, concerned with the nature of family life in his home country, was determined to attack the problem of 'Mixed Marriage as Practised in Indonesia', concentrating on the pastoral aspects. Indonesia is a secular state and pluralist in terms of ethnic groups, where the law concerning mixed marriages is interpreted in one way by the Supreme Court and in another way by the Minister of Interior

Affairs. The researcher discusses these approaches and the response of the Christian Church and other bodies. Some churches prohibit their members from having a mixed marriage; some recognize it between churches, but prohibit mixed marriages between different religions; while others recognize both kinds of mixed marriages, provided that the non-Christian party is willing to attend church and be instructed. Pastors have a particular role to play in this context. They should advise those concerned regarding matters directly spiritual, that is, present scriptural principles to the party concerned, the possibility of back-sliding in the case of the Christian partner, and the effect on the children. The non-Christian should be expected to attend church and not hinder the Christian party from doing so. Physical aspects should be considered, such as sexual relationships and eating customs. Both aspects, spiritual and physical, should be considered in the church context, as they are aspects of oversight and discipline. Another important role for the pastors is to act as a pressure group as far as the Government is concerned. They should, according to the researcher, follow the example of those who influenced the authorities in 1945 and prevented Indonesia from becoming an Islamic state. Towards the close of the work some helpful insights are given on relevant scriptural passages, including, 1 Corinthians 5:9-10, 10:27, 2 Corinthians 6:14, Leviticus 19:19, Deuteronomy 7:3-4 and 27:21.

The discussions concerning the Diploma/Degree Course continued, cautiously, from 1987 to 1989. Mr Clem Roberts was a Deputy Director of the Polytechnic of Wales, Pontypridd, and a member of the

College Council. Mr Roberts and the members of staff explored the possibilities informally and it was a tremendous help that he could wear two hats at the same time.[10] A positive step was taken when the Principal visited Pontypridd, followed by a deputation from the Polytechnic to the College.[11] Some time lapsed before concrete suggestions were made. The possibilities were, (a) not to implement any changes and keep to the status quo, (b) associate directly with CNAA, Council for National Academic Awards, and introduce changes through that body, or, (c) associate with the Polytechnic either on a part-time basis or in full collaboration. There was a favourable response to the third possibility, but it was felt that more detailed information was needed relating to the suggested relationship before a full discussion could take place and before any decisions could be made.[12] The Principal paid another visit to Pontypridd and reported that the next step would be for the staff to prepare a draft proposal for the consideration of the Director of the Polytechnic.[13]

Mr Clem Roberts prepared the staff for a further meeting with representatives of the Polytechnic, which was held on 19 March 1990, and a report from that meeting was discussed by the staff, College president and chairman of the College Council. One need which emerged from that meeting was for someone to take the lead, to advise and facilitate arrangements. Mr Clem Roberts' name was put forward, and he was met by representatives of the College Council who invited him to be Accreditation Secretary, an appointment which was endorsed by the full College Council.[14] The Accreditation Secretary committed himself wholeheartedly to his work, while the members of staff settled down to prepare their respective courses and to interact in staff meetings.

Interaction clarified the rationale for a validated course. There was absolute agreement that whatever changes would take place there would be no compromise with respect to the Word of God: 'The College will withdraw immediately from these discussions if it considers that its aims or its theology are threatened *in any way.*'[15] It was in the light of this conviction that the Principal advocated a positive approach:[16]

Because we take the New Testament warnings about false teaching seriously, College tutors have a responsibility to acquaint a new generation of preachers/missionaries with the basic presuppositions, arguments and devastating conclusions of the critics.

This responsibility relates:

a)   to the prevailing climate of thought in which these students will minister. In our churches, many young people imbibe critical theories in schools/colleges, while adults hear/read about such theories regularly in the media/ books

b)   Our students will need to be able to warn both young and old concerning such theories and expose them in a responsible manner, e.g., Titus 1:7, c.f., the threat of Gnosticism in the New Testament Church

c)   In preaching there is inevitably some interaction with unbelieving, secular ideas, not only for apologetic purposes but also for positive and meaningful communication of the Truth.

Such an approach did not mean that the staff would think of their teaching as being open-ended. Instruction would still be given on the basis of faith, but other views, not evangelical, would be considered responsibly. The believing man is a thinking man and there is no need for the believer to be ashamed of his evangelical convictions.

The mind must be subjected to God, and that happens by coming under the authority of the Word of God. The written Word must be considered under the guidance of the Holy Spirit, and the Word must be preached. The College endeavours to honour the Word in terms of actual preaching, exegesis and exposition and in the course on homiletics. This is central in the thinking of the College. In terms of conveying the truth, it is generally acknowledged that there are many ways of doing so, as is evident from the ministry of the Lord Jesus Christ and the apostle Paul. They adopted the question and answer approach, visual aids and the debating method.

The Principal in his statement related this approach to the theme of common grace, as Dr Cook had done in his lecture on the nature of research work. In the course of his argument, Dr Davies quoted P. E. Hughes to confirm his argument:[17]

To common grace, then, we must thankfully attribute God's continuing care of His creation, as He provides for the needs of His creatures, restrains human society from becoming altogether intolerable and ungovernable, and makes it possible for mankind, though fallen, to live together in a generally orderly and co-operative manner; to show neutral forbearance, and to cultivate together the scientific, cultural, and economic pursuits of civilization.

Despite man's total depravity, co-operation between believers and unbelievers in society, including education, is possible because of common grace. All changes, however, had to be considered carefully, and in no way would they be allowed to marr the worshipping, devotional ethos and the doctrinal stand of the College.

A formal resolution was made on 5 December 1990: 'It is decided to proceed with accreditation and validation with the Polytechnic of Wales and the Council is looking to the staff to support this decision.' One member of staff strongly dissented from the resolution and gave his reasons clearly, and forcibly: (a) he felt that there would be compromise on the biblical teaching involved in the training for the ministry, (b) he did not believe that the theology board of the Polytechnic of Wales would accredit the kind of course ETCW would present, and that therefore a lot of time and money would have been spent unnecessarily.[18] Sadly, the Rev. John Cook could not comply with College policy and this meant the end of his ministry at the College, a ministry which had started in 1966, consistently characterized by dedication and zeal. Generations of students will always be grateful to him for his patience in teaching them Greek, not just as a language, but as a means of understanding the message of the New Testament.

The staff continued to grapple with the demands of the changes, and met regularly for many a long hour. A Course Board was set up comprising all members of staff, with Noel Gibbard as chairman. Almost immediately they were joined by the visiting lecturers and two student representatives, and their contributions enriched the discussions. The main functions of the Board were: 1. To implement relevant policies of the Academic Board relating to the conduct of courses, 2. To undertake the related activities of monitoring and evaluation established by the Academic Board, 3. To make recommendations to the Academic Board regarding developments in the content or the conduct of the course.[19] The Course Board was fortunate to have the continuing advice of Dr David Cook, Oxford, as he had considerable experience in the realm of theological education. He spent the best part of the day at the College on 24 May 1991. He was satisfied with the content of the course and the criticisms he offered were aimed at 'presentation' and the 'tone' of what was said. The staff looked in detail at his suggestions and prepared the final draft for the authorities at Pontypridd.

The Polytechnic of Wales asked the College to revise the proposed course and present it again the following year. Although there was initial disappointment, there is no doubt that it was the correct decision, as it gave more time to look at detail and also gave the staff the opportunity to teach the course for one year while working on revision at the same time. The Diploma was validated in 1992. The course was divided into six components: Old Testament, New Testament, Church History, Theology, Missiology and Pastoral Studies. They were subdivided into a number of different subjects. When the third-year degree course was introduced the linear system was changed into a modular one, which involved the staff in a great deal of work, but the task was accomplished in a comparatively short time. There were some teething problems, but staff and students soon settled down and since 1993 many lessons have been learnt, which have led to a number of revisions. This is a continuing exercise. Both courses are included in an appendix and will give an insight into the subjects covered at the College.

Apart from working on the research programme and the degree course, the College felt that it should respond to the demand for a correspondence course. Letters of enquiry revealed that many people would like the opportunity to study at home.[20] A prepared plan would help them to discipline themselves and benefit from regular study. Only five units were prepared to start the new venture, consisting of eight lessons each. By the end of 1989, 35 persons had enrolled, which increased to 95 by the middle of 1991. Persons of all kinds of background and occupations have showed interest. Apart from a number of housewives and unemployed the early list included a pastor, teacher, welder, fishmonger, pharmacist, plumber, postman, police inspector, die sinker, trained solicitor and an airline pilot.

The application is usually made by an individual, but there are a few examples of husband and wife sharing the study together, and two or three examples of a request by an individual intending to introduce the study into the local church. A husband was enjoying the study when he was taken suddenly to be with his Lord. In deep anguish the widow's faith was tested, but one of the helps she received was taking the course which her late husband had enjoyed so much. Another married couple were converted but were having doctrinal problems. They heard Dr Martyn Lloyd-Jones speaking on tape on Romans chapter 3, which provided them with a basis to think doctrinally. They applied to follow the course in order to be confirmed in the faith. A number of people want to be helped in terms of evangelism, acknowledging that they cannot speak effectively to others without a clear understanding of the basic truths of Scripture. A Czechoslovakian, working in Germany, was helped personally and this encouraged him to find means to send the gospel into his native country.

Some of those following the course have very little doctrinal knowledge, while others are quite advanced. A glowing example of a dedicated student was the married man from Hampshire. He was informed of the ETCW Correspondence Course by a friend, who soon afterwards died. The married man had such a thirst for knowledge that he arranged to visit a retired pastor once a week in order to be advised by an experienced person, and was most glad when the first unit of the study course arrived. He was unemployed at the time, but even taking this into consideration, he must have been a voracious reader, because the last ten books he had read were, Martyn Lloyd-Jones on Romans 8:5-17; Whitefield's *Sermons*; Flavel, *Mystery of Providence*; Thomas Brooks, *Heaven on Earth*; Calvin, *Sermons from Job*; Pink, *The Sovereignty of God*; Kuiper, *The Glorious Body of Christ*; James Stewart, *A Man in Christ*; Campbell Morgan, *The Crises of the Christ*; Hope, *Life of C. H. Spurgeon*; Thomas Manton, *John 17* and J. C. Ryle, *Holiness*.

All the home countries are represented in the

applications, with a good number from Scotland. Germany has been mentioned already, and there was an unusual request from Belgium, from a person who not only asked for some of the units but also advice on how to learn Welsh. So far the College has not received any of her answers in the language of heaven. There have been enquiries from France, Catalonia and Italy. How refreshing it was to receive a letter from a person who has visited the College, working as an evangelist in Hungary, with the opening paragraph:[21]

The warm weather has finally arrived here, and the early cherries are turning from blushing pink to mouth-watering red. How wonderfully has the Lord Creator made the world! We have not only been given these useful things, the things we need, but they are also pleasing to the eye, and speak not only of the God of power but of beauty.

I find his Word is the same: not only is it useful for our lives but beautiful to the spiritual eyes. As a ripening cherry makes the mouth water, so does the glory of His word make one hungry for more.

Altogether, during the early years, the enquiries and applications came from ten countries.

Letters have come from further afield, from America, Ghana, Nigeria, and a word has been received from an UFM missionary in Papua, New Guinea, expressing her appreciation of the lessons. A lay preacher from New Zealand was following a course in a particular college but was dissatisfied with the teaching, sent for the ETCW course and asked a local minister to be his supervisor. A sales executive from Western Australia had started preaching with the blessing of the church which had just been formed in

1982, standing firmly on the Baptist Confession of
1689. He covered a number of units faithfully and
diligently.

The correspondence course has reached the home,
the church and the missionary campus, but it has
also reached the prison, two of them at home and
one abroad. One of the prisoners was converted just
two months after being interred, and immediately
had an appetite for reading the Scriptures and books
explaining the faith. In a very short time he had a
firm grasp of the basic doctrines of the Bible and
continued to study regularly. During his stay in
prison he was visited by a student from the College
and was most appreciative of the visits and the
course. In his letters he expressed real joy because he
was able to study, 'I really look forward to the arrival
of the course and being guided in a strict, sound doctrinal study'. All the time possible was spent in the
education department and he was most disappoin-
ted when that centre closed down. The reading of
the prisoner included the IVP's Dictionary; Packer,
Knowing God; Bruce, *The Spreading Flame*; Berkhof,
Systematic Theology and Hendriksen, *Gospel of John*.
In one letter he related how he had been challenged
by Packer's question, 'Do you really know your God?'

A Nigerian, from a well-educated family, was sentenced to eight years imprisonment in Thailand, but
while he was there he was converted through the
witness of Prison Fellowship. A friend sponsored
him to follow the correspondence course, and the
prisoner did so with enthusiasm. In order to have
peace and quiet he would study from one to five o'
clock in the morning, and would write extensive

answers. Occasionally he had difficulty with the prison authorities who would refuse to censor and post his mail. In spite of all opposition the imprisoned, but free man, continued steadfast in the faith.[22]

These are only a few examples of the large number who have followed, and who are following, the course. During one period from 1994 to 1995 there were over 230 enquiries and applications. It is also encouraging that a few who have followed the correspondence course have been led to the College to study on a full-time basis.

The College and the churches

The ranks of the teaching staff were strengthened by the coming of permanent tutors and visits of pastors. The Rev. Iwan Rhys Jones came to the College just in time to take part in the discussions on the Diploma/ Degree Course. He had pastored a Welsh Congregational Church in Fishguard, Dyfed, and spent some time as assistant to the Rev. Peter Milsom at Deeside before coming to Bryntirion. His meticulous care for detail made him the ideal person to be the registrar, when Mr Clem Roberts moved to be pastor of Mount Pleasant Baptist Church, Swansea. The Rev. Trevor Burke from Northern Ireland lectured for a brief period but felt constrained to return to his native Ulster, and the Rev. Tom Holland, Letchworth, Hertfordshire, began on a part-time basis before being appointed full-time in 1993. He had eighteen years experience as a pastor of an FIEC Church, but at the time of his coming to Bryntirion was pursuing research work. The other full-time tutor, Dr Tom Gledhill from Bristol, but Lincolnshire born, was also appointed in 1993. He had taken a doctorate in physics, and studied theology, before spending twenty years in Africa, six of them as a lecturer in an Anglican Evangelical College in Nairobi, Kenya.

There was a loss, as well as additions, with the sudden homecall of the Rev. Hugh D. Morgan, Malpas, Newport, a Council member, and a visiting lecturer until 1989. During the March 1992 Council Meeting, members were given an opportunity to express acknowledgement of his service and leadership, which can be summarized in the words of the Council minute: 'His godly, humble, wise, gentle and gracious pastoral influence within his church and the College here will be sorely missed and much thanks is due to God for the life and ministry of this man.'

The students continued to come and some details concerning them will illustrate the growth and the nature of the student body.[23]

Students, June 1991

Student Body: 49, 43 following the Diploma Course and 6 research students.Men: 34, Women: 9; 26 Married, 17 Single.

Nationality: 43 Diploma Students:

Home Countries	33	Nigeria	2
Zambia	3	Israel	1
Romania	3	Germany	1

Age:

19–25 years	13	41–45	5
26–30	12	46–50	3
31–35	4	51 +	1
36–40	5		

A survey of the students four years later (1994–95), reveals similarities and significant developments:[24]

Student Body: 52 [53 in September 1994, but one student left]
Undergraduates and College Course
Male: 42, Female: 10
Married couples: 3, Engaged to be married: 2

Nationality:

England	19	Korea	4
Wales	13	Poland	1
Scotland	2	Ethiopia	1
Northern Ireland	1	Siberia	1
Ghana	2	Zambia	2
Romania	2	Italy	2
Nigeria	1	Ukraine	1

Home Countries: 35, Overseas: 17

There was a marked increase in the number of countries represented, and the overseas students made up almost half of the student body.

The first group of students gained their BA Honours Degree in 1994 and the results were very encouraging:[25]

Total 14
    Class 2 (i): 8, Class 2 (ii): 3, Class 3: 2, Ordinary Degree: 1
    Of the 14 students, 7 have been employed as Church Ministers/Assistants, 5 in the UK, and 2 overseas
    4 students are doing postgraduate studies at the College
    1 is pursuing a PGCE at Trinity College, Carmarthen
    1 exploring possibilities

One promising student, Peter Morgan, had expected to go with his wife, also a student, and child to Brazil to be involved in Theological Education by Extension, but was tragically killed in a climbing accident.

That was the situation in September 1994, but apart from the graduates and the undergraduates

there were 25 postgraduates, which increased by
September 1995 to 35.

A number of steps have been taken to confirm the
relationship between the College and the churches in
the area and far afield. The College was brought into
being to serve the churches and there is no meaning
to its existence apart from them. One fairly recent
development has strengthened the links. Representatives from different church groupings have been invited on to the College Council, and they are, the
Associated Churches EMW, EFCC, FIEC and Grace
Baptist Churches. Also, meetings with church representatives have proved to be fruitful. Since 1990 pastors and other leaders of churches have gathered at
Bryntirion to see the College for themselves and to
share meaningfully concerning the students. Twenty
churches were represented in 1993, with apologies
from four other churches. The discussion, led by Dr
Davies, was based on two draft documents, 'Relationship between Students' Home Church and
ETCW', and 'Some Guidelines for a Students' Home
Church'.[26] Many helpful points were made concerning the church's response to the care of a student, including presenting his needs in the prayer meeting
at least once a month, have one person with a particular interest in the student, have someone to write to
him regularly and have the student on placement at
the home church once during his stay at the College.
Further meetings were held in 1994 and 1995, led by
the Rev. Elwyn Davies, the College president, and
apart from representatives of churches who had students in the College, others interested in the work

were also present. All those who have taken part in these discussions are anxious for them to continue.

Links with local churches are vitally important. The College appreciates the close relationship with Ogmore Vale and Llangeinor, both pastors being former students, and with Freeschool Court, Bridgend, whose pastor is a visiting lecturer, and the group of Presbyterian churches in the Rhondda, whose pastor also visited the College for a number of years. The same close relationship is enjoyed with Maesteg; Ogmore-by-sea; Gilgal, Porthcawl; and Litchard, Bridgend. Some of the students have been engaged in pioneering work at Brackla, and, more recently, others have joined the young church on that estate. Pastorless churches like Laleston and Blackmill have been most appreciative of the contribution of the students, and they in turn have gained much experience for their future work.

Declining causes have also benefited from the persevering work of the students. A small church in Rhoose had almost closed, but after a period of preaching and visiting it was possible for one of the mature students to have an oversight of the cause. In Maerdy, Rhondda Fach, the few faithful members were concerned as to what would happen in the immediate future. One of the Bryntirion students settled down there for one year in an unofficial capacity, but led the faithful in preaching, prayer and Bible study. Interest was renewed, and soon after the student left it was possible for the church to call a pastor, who is now following the degree course, part-time, at the College. This is most encouraging, especially in the Rhondda, where so many churches are closing and being turned to storehouses and places of entertainment. A few of the students are thinking seriously of working with declining causes or in pioneering situations.

Most of the students who come to the College follow a validated course, but there are other possibilities, and a few come for one year and some come just for a few terms. The brief stays have been truly appreciated, especially by missionaries. A missionary couple, with eleven years experience in South Africa, expressed their feelings after one term at the College: 'We are very grateful for all the work done by the teaching staff to bring the truths of Scripture into focus and to bear on our everyday ministry. We appreciated the fellowship with staff and students, and also the emphasis on prayer which is so evident in the life of the College. In attending the College for one term we were looking for spiritual refreshment and a deeper insight into God's Word, and the Lord graciously met those needs'.[27] In the light of their experience they made positive suggestions to improve the Missiology course. They pointed out the imbalance in the time allocated to different aspects of the course, and the fact that not all relevant issues had been included. The College was able to learn from them, as well as their being able to learn from the College.

A few have come just for one year in order to concentrate on a particular aspect of Christian work. Recently, Steven Levy left the College to work with his home church, Lôn-las, near Skewen, burdened by the condition of the youngsters who were completely outside the church, and with great patience and love he continues to work with that group of people. At times he has experienced verbal and physical opposition, but the work has been blessed and a good number of youngsters have been converted. They come to a discipleship class on a Saturday afternoon to be built up in their faith. On Sunday night there is an open meeting for young people at 8 pm, which is a simple preaching service. Converts, and those interested in the gospel, are given Bible notes prepared by the former student and checked by Dr Davies. These notes are also used in other places, especially in Barry, where the evangelist works in conjunction with Bethel Baptist Church, and for a brief period was helped by Robert Owen, another Bryntirion student.

Not only does Steve work in the home church itself, and that with the blessing of the church, he also works in a pioneering situation nearby. He himself refers to this aspect of the work: 'The biggest part of my work is planting a church in Birchgrove (an area near to Lôn-las). We started the work last October [1994], and now have a Sunday night service each week where between 30 and 50 attend. I usually preach. We also hold a bible study/prayer meeting on Tuesday night. They also come to my home for coffee once a week.'[28] It is wonderful to witness such zeal and to know that God is blessing his word to the salvation of many.

With his pastor, and others, the Christian worker should make sure that his principles for undertaking the work are clear and scriptural. The basic conviction is that God alone is able to save. He must work in the hearts of sinners in order to bring them to himself. Consequently, God's work must be done in

God's way, and therefore no gimmicks should be used in order to draw people to Christ. There must be flexibility and informality to some extent, but in terms of the content of the message, Christ crucified must be at the centre. There is a great need for such pioneering work both at home and abroad.

The College and the world

Continuing efforts were made to confirm existing links with overseas countries and establish new ones. Kenya was not forgotten and in 1986 Peniel Evangelical Church, Maesteg, brought over Pastor John, followed a year later by Washington Were, supported by Horsell Evangelical Church, pastored by the Rev. Ian Childs, a former student. The hand of God's providence has opened up the way for many unexpected students to come to the College. From 1990 until 1995 students have come from Romania, Ukraine, Poland, Siberia, Italy and Pakistan.

The relationship with Romania was established by Josef Tson and Les Tidball (Romania Missionary Society), who asked the College to receive three students, Alex Niagoi, Adrian Popa and Cornell Ghita. This was made possible by the overthrow of Ceausescu's regime in December 1989. When the three were invited to come the decision was a difficult one to make, because they could not speak English. The Baptist Seminary they attended was anxious to keep them, and two of them were married. They decided to come and were met at Heathrow by Mr Alan Penrose of Cardiff (RMS), on 14 October 1990. The main problem was that of language, making it difficult for them to follow the lectures, but they made good progress and at the end of the first term were able to follow ninety per cent of what was being said. Alex moved to London, but Adrian and Cornell were joined, first, by Maria and then in 1994, by Beny, the last two being married in August 1995. Adrian continues the story:[29]

Also in 1994 Cornell and I came to the end of our four-year pilgrimage in Wales. We could thank the Lord for all we have learned and experienced here and look forward to serving Him and his people at home. But while Cornell felt that the Lord was primarily calling him to minister to a particular church in Romania (Chisianu Cris), I decided to attempt further preparation for a more academic task. And this is what I do at the moment, writing a thesis in the area of wisdom literature in partial fulfilment for an M.Phil degree. God willing, I shall finish next June [1996], and then start teaching OT at the Western University of Timisoara in Romania.

Oleg Dolina, from the Ukraine, tragically lost his family in a road accident, and had to leave the college he was attending in Yugoslavia, when trouble started in that country. Friends in Nantwich put him in touch with the College in Bryntirion. Like Oleg, Jerzy Siciarz from Poland, is a research student, and both of them would like to do translation work, as they see the need of good Christian literature in the native languages of their people. Edward Kovalyov has come from Siberia, and, like the others, is glad to be in the College, rejoicing with them in the saving grace of the gospel. His story reminds us of the irresistible, saving and keeping grace of God:[30]

My conversion is basically a story of my coming to understand the power of God. Ironically enough, gaining power was the main purpose of my life and the only thing which gave meaning to my existence. Up to the point of my conversion my entire life was governed by the principle, 'The big fish eats the small one. The bigger you are the better your capacity to swallow. And you are getting bigger by swallowing small fishes.' That was the simple philosophy of my life, and everything in the world was of secondary and relative importance. I used all possible means to gain more power and influence. I was involved in the world of crime and violence, and led a life of double standards. I was ruthless and immoral, but thought I was right because all the world around me was evil.

My philosophy, however, ran into trouble. My conscience started to control my will. It seemed that my conscience was just an instrument in the hands of somebody standing behind it, and that somebody was incredibly powerful and intelligent. Who was that somebody? Slowly I came to call him God, and wanted to know more about him. I decided to do something practical, which was, to go to the Russian Orthodox Church. My first impression was that I was near the answer I was looking for, but soon realised that it was not so as I got tired of the ritual and calling upon the saints. I almost lost hope, but suddenly had a desire to get hold of a New Testament. I obtained one in spite of many difficulties, my wife's objection, the cost, which was a month's salary, and, of course, the Scriptures were forbidden literature.

While reading the New Testament, I made some astonishing discoveries. Contrary to my expectation the central theme of the book was the Lord Jesus Christ, not the saints of the Russian Orthodox Church, and that person claimed to be God in the flesh. Here, I thought, was super power, which I admired, but when I came to the account of the crucifixion, I had to change my mind. Indeed, I was shocked. Here was one, who claimed to be God, being crucified by evil men. Had he lost his divine power? In meditating on the cross I realised that here was the manifestation of the greatest power in the world, the love of God to sinners. That love had reached me and had averted the wrath of God from falling on my sin. I was filled with fear and love at the same time.

There was no doubt that the power of God's love had changed me. That was the last day for me to be governed by the principle of worldly power because I was captivated by the spiritual power of the love of God.

A few days after that remarkable event, I read the words written by the apostle Paul so many years ago, 'For the message of the cross is foolishness to those who are perishing, but to us who are being saved it is the power of God', 1 Corinthians 1:18. How great was that power which saved me!

A very different country from Siberia is Korea, in terms of culture, wealth and the Protestant traditon. Jong Tae Lee, one of the students from that country, has finished his course in the College, and he now represents it in Romania and Asia. He arranged Dr Davies' first visit to Korea in 1991, and Dr Davies himself refers to his impressions of that visit: 'I was profoundly challenged in 1991—the great love of believers, their emphasis on prayer, prayer mountains, meeting Pastors whose fathers (Pastors), had been imprisoned and shot by the communists in the North, hearing from key leaders of the burden of prayer they had in the 60s and 70s for revival and evangelism and hearing how God answered.'[31] Dr Davies concentrated on visiting Presbyterian Churches and Seminaries, and preached in churches belonging to four of the five Presbyterian denominations. He did preach in one independent church, which had its own professional soccer team, all the players being believers and church members.

Dr Davies also referred to the missionary outlook of the churches: 'The missionary burden of many churches was astonishing; I have never met such universal church concern for world mission.'[32] They

The new building—part of the premises of ETCW, Bryntirion. Bryntirion conference centre, which incorporates the new college wing and additional student accommodation and lecture rooms, is out of view behind and to the right.

are involved in Japan, Indonesia, the Philippines, Thailand and China. There are two million Korean Chinese in Manchuria and the church there is growing rapidly. Some missionaries have gone to Russia, and many are waiting for North Korea to open so that they might take the gospel there. Dr Davies' second visit of 1992 was very helpful in terms of preaching and visiting seminaries. By 1993 he felt much at home and had greater freedom in preaching. The 1994 visit was the highlight in consolidating relationships. During these visits the Principal has made a number of valuable contributions to theological conferences, including the International Symposium in Soong Sil University, Seoul. His articles have appeared in *Ministry and Theology*, a journal which is read by twelve thousand church leaders.

Blessing is always accompanied by dangers. The church in Korea is troubled with the presence of sects and exaggerated charismatic claims. When Dr Davies was there in 1992 many were expecting the Second Coming of the Lord Jesus Christ, and were bewildered when it did not take place. Secularization is affecting many churches and older pastors are concerned about some of the younger pastors and teachers. The links and the interaction between the College and Korea can contribute to the growth of sound doctrine and spiritual outlook in both the institution and the country. Students are still coming from Korea as undergraduates and postgraduates, and part of their education is to visit Hanover Chapel in Gwent, where the Rev. Robert Thomas was brought up, the LMS pioneer missionary who was killed in North Korea.

The Indonesian student, mentioned in the section on research work, went back home burdened by the need in his own land. It is not possible to know the exact number of Christians in Indonesia, but it would be between twenty and forty million; yet, that would only be between ten and twenty per cent of the population. The country experienced revival during the 1970s, creating a greater need for teachers and pastors to build up the faith of the believers. There is also a need to combat false teaching because about half of the seminaries are influenced by liberal theology. The Indonesian is determined to do as much as possible to help his fellow countrymen. His heart's desire and prayer for them is that they might be saved.

The student graduate was faced with a number of possibilities, especially in the context of Bible teaching. He could return to teach at the seminary where he himself was taught, join a church which was considering opening a new Bible college or lecture in another college from January 1996. He was convinced, however, that something had to be done immediately, and in conjunction with a church in the capital city he formed the Open Bible Institute to train lay leaders to work in the churches and in a wider Christian ministry. It is hoped that a seminary in the city will work with the church, and if this does happen, it will be possible to extend the course to a wider area. The plan meets with the needs of a good number of people who cannot follow a full-time course in a college. In forming the course the Indonesian has depended heavily on the Bryntirion, ETCW programme, and a more official relationship could develop between the College and the Open Bible Institute.[33]

The staff try to keep in touch with developments in ministerial training by attending conferences and other colleges. Two helpful visits have been paid to Oak Hill Theological College, London, where it was possible to share and compare notes with fellow workers. A most significant development has taken place recently in the Highlands of Scotland, with which the ETCW is glad to be associated. On 15 September 1994 representatives of the Highland Theological Institute visited Bryntirion. They were in the process of setting up a theological college in Elgin, which was to be accommodated within Moray College of Further Education. The aim was to establish an independent, evangelical and reformed Theological College. They were teaching the Cambridge Diploma in Religious Studies, but wanted to develop a BA course and a research programme. As a result of discussions with Bryntirion and the University of Glamorgan, the Highland Institute was granted the right to teach the Bryntirion course; that is, it is regarded as a 'franchised degree of the University of Glamorgan'. A friendly relationship has been established between Elgin and Bryntirion, and both colleges share a common burden in terms of doctrine, ministerial preparation and revival. God willing, joint staff conferences will be held annually.

Reflections

Bryntirion can be regarded as God's signpost. It points to the known past and to the unknown future.

ETCW group photo, 1994–5. *From left to right*: Peter Milsom, Tom Holland, Iwan Rhys Jones, Chris Connor, Philip Ross, Eryl Davies, Noel Gibbard, Tom Gledhill, Elvira Henry, Valérie Fanguin, Iola Thomas, Malcolm Jones

In looking to the past it is possible to see the hand of God leading, preserving and overruling. One message comes clearly through the blessings and difficulties of sixty years, and can be summarized in the words of the prophet Zechariah, 'Despise not the day of small things' (4:10). What is seen in Bryntirion today started as a Bible class in a Rhondda vestry. The small stone has become a mountain, and the acorn has become a tree. At times it seemed as if the stone and the acorn would be crushed, especially during the period 1949 to 1951, but much grace was given to Mr Fidler to continue.

During all the years from Porth to Bryntirion, many differences emerge and many mistakes were made. Occasionally, doctrinal issues caused problems, and sometimes personal tensions hindered the work. There are also examples of wrong staff appointments having been made. It is crucial to have the right men to teach in an evangelical, theological college.

Yet, in spite of all these drawbacks, many things unite the three periods. First and foremost, there was an unflinching adherence to the Scriptures as the inspired, infallible Word of God. The Bible, for staff and students, was the Word of God written. Whatever the differences might have been in terms of holiness and prophecy, the Word of God was the final authority.

Secondly, the Word of God has been applied, in terms of ministry at home and abroad. Men have been, and are trained, to be pastors, able to preach the gospel. A high percentage of students have become pastors and teachers in Britain and many countries of

the world. Also, men, and women, have been prepared for different aspects of Christian service, and
the College has always welcomed women to equip
them for a particular vocation. Over 90% of the students become pastors, evangelists or missionaries
abroad, compared with 24% in the LBC. In terms of
the sphere of ministry, the world has been a parish
for the College. There have been deficiencies in the
Missiology course, and there is room for improvement as far as the present one is concerned, but the
world-wide vision has never been lost throughout
the history of the College.

Thirdly, there has been a concern for revival. There
has been an apostolic succession in this context. Mr
Fidler knew R. B. Jones, and both experienced the
Revival of 1904; John Waite knew Mr Fidler and Eryl
Davies knows John Waite. The first two mentioned
tasted God's grace in an exceptional way, but the
stone cast in 1904 had ripples later in Barry and now
in Bryntirion. The phenomenon of revival has an important place in the teaching and the prayer life of
the College. It is imperative to make the teaching
clear, especially in the context of so much confusion
in our day, but with the teaching there must be a
prayerful spirit, which must be cultivated under the
ministry of the Holy Spirit himself. Bryntirion—
which means 'pleasant hill'—would be a pleasant
hill indeed if the Spirit of God were to visit us like
the sound of a rushing wind. We do desire to see the
days of the right hand of God. This burden is shared
by the Evangelical Movement of Wales, and it is fit-
ting that the work of the College is being developed
on the Bryntirion site. The Movement's concern for

God's work through the College has been expressed in prayer and practical considerations, not least in the terms of the lease given on the property. It is good for brethren to dwell together in unity, especially when there is so much disunity in the evangelical world.

Fourthly, each Principal had to face the challenge of social, theological and educational changes. One distinctive way in which Bryntirion has been able to do so, is to be an independent, reformed theological College and be able to provide the students, if they so wish, with a BA degree course. The educational changes, however, are controlled by the teaching of the College and its prayerful spirit.

The signpost points to the future. There are clear tokens of God's goodness. There is an increase in the number of students, with a total, including the research students, of ninety in September 1995. The new wing was opened on 23 November 1995, and there are plans to extend the College building. All concerned with the College are very conscious that it is God alone who can sustain and prosper the work. We go forward with our confidence in him. We stand on the Scriptures alone, proclaim justification by faith alone and that to the glory of God alone. May God be pleased to bless the work of many generations of students, and grant persevering grace to the servants of the Word. May many more be prepared to serve the glorious gospel of our great God.

REFERENCES

1. Council Minutes, 19 October, 19 November 1984; information Dr Davies.
2. Letter, 3 May 1995.
3. 'A Brief Report', 10 December 1987.
4. Comments taken from students' diaries.
5. 'Students' Wives Draft Discussion', drawn up by Dr Davies.
6. Council Minutes, 7 December 1987.
7. Delivered 5 March 1995; some of the content discussed on previous occasions.
8. Ibid.
9. Ibid.
10. Faculty Meeting, 6 November 1987.
11. Ibid., 19 December 1987.
12. Ibid., 13 April 1989, Council Minutes, 30 June 1989.
13. Council Minutes, 11 September 1989.
14. Started work 1 April 1989.
15. News Letter, April 1991.
16. 'Validation and Orthodoxy', drawn up by Dr Davies, discussed by the staff, 26 November and by the Council, 5 December 1990.
17. Ibid.
18. Council Minutes, 29 June 1990.
19. Document: Proposed Diploma of Higher Education in Theological Studies, 1991, 40.
20. Council Minutes, 7 December 1987.
21. Letter, 25 May 1994.
22. Correspondence kept at Bryntirion.
23. Proposed Diploma, op. cit., 6-7.
24. Monitoring Report, 1994–5.
25. Ibid.
26. Minutes, 24 November 1993.
27. Letter, Victor and Rachel Fredlund, 14 April 1993.
28. Information from Steve Levy.
29. Information from Adrian Popa.
30. Provided by Edward Kovalyov.
31. Information provided by Dr Davies.
32. Ibid.
33. Reports from Tjeng Sam Him.

Appendices

A. DOCTRINAL BASIS, ETCW

We accept the Holy Scriptures, as originally given, as the inspired, infallible and inerrant word of God. Recognizing them as the sole authority in all matters of faith and practice, we believe the doctrines taught therein. In particular we believe:

1. in the only true and living God, the Holy Trinity of Divine Persons in perfect unity, immutable, co-equal, co-eternal, Father, Son and Holy Spirit, and sovereign in creation, providence and redemption.

2. in the God and Father of our Lord Jesus Christ, who is holy, righteous, full of grace and love. In His infinite love He sent forth the Son, that the world through Him might be saved.

3. in the Lord Jesus Christ, the only incarnate Son of God, born of the Virgin Mary, conceived by the Holy Spirit, in consequence of which His manhood was real and sinless, and His teaching free from error; that by His death on the Cross He made substitutionary atonement and a perfect offering for sins; that He triumphed over death, sin and Satan; that He rose bodily from the grave, ascended into heaven, where He now sits at the right hand of God.

4. in the Holy Spirit, the third Person of the Godhead, and the Agent of regeneration, by whom men are brought to conviction, repentance, and faith in the Lord Jesus Christ, and who indwells the believer for sanctification. The Holy Spirit guides the worship and ministry of the church, and empowers its life and witness.

5. that as a result of the Fall human nature became guilty and depraved, so that all men are subject to the penalty which, in His wrath, God has decreed against sin. Notwithstanding, those who remain impenitent are fully responsible for their wilful continuance in sin and unbelief.

6. that through faith alone in the Lord Jesus Christ, and on the basis of His death, the sinners are freely justified by God, who forgives all their sins as they are reckoned to Christ, whose righteousness is reckoned to them. Salvation is therefore by grace, and not by human merit or work.

241

7. that those who are chosen by God the Father and redeemed by the blood of the Lord Jesus Christ and sanctified by the Holy Spirit are members of the universal Church, the body of which Christ is head. This Church finds visible expression in local churches, each of whom should manifest union with Christ in preserving purity of life and doctrine, avoiding schism and heresy.

8. that the Lord Jesus Christ will return visibly, and personally in power and glory. That there is to be a resurrection and final judgement of all men, issuing in eternal blessedness for believers and eternal punishment for the wicked.

B. THE COLLEGE COURSE

1960–85

Some changes were made during these years, but the course was basically the same throughout the period:

DETAILS OF CURRICULUM

The curriculum is planned on a three-year basis. A, B and C courses run concurrently. Students may apply for a two-year course which would normally comprise courses A and B. In certain special circumstances students are admitted for a one-year course comprising of elements from A, B and C courses. This is usually available only to mature students who have already been engaged in some form of Christian service.

'A' Year

Old Testament Introduction and Content
New Testament Introduction and Content
Bible Exegesis: Three Old Testament Books
                Three New Testament Books
Early Church History
Systematic Theology: Scripture, God and the Holy Spirit, Man
Biblical Hebrew
New Testament Greek
Principles of Homiletics
Missionary Studies
All students with the necessary aptitude are expected to commence Hebrew in their second term.

'B' Year

Bible Exegesis: Six Old Testament books

Three New Testament books

Reformation Church History

Systematic Theology: The Person of Christ, The Work of Christ, Grace

The Period Between the Testaments

An Introduction to General Hermeneutics

Textual Criticism and Canon of Scripture

Hebrew Grammar and detailed study of selected portions of the Hebrew Text

Greek: Gospel of John (detailed study of the Greek Text)

Pastorolia and Practical Homiletics

Missionary Studies

'C' Year

Bible Exegesis: Six Old Testament books

Three New Testament books

Systematic Theology: The Church and Eschatology

Christian Ethics

Modern Church History

Principles of Prophetic Interpretation and the Apocalypse

Hebrew (detailed study of selected portions of the Old Testament, e.g. Judges, Joel and Psalms)

Greek: 1 Corinthians (detailed study of the Greek Text)

Practical Homiletics

Missionary Studies.

1985-92

The course was, basically, that taught at Barry; changes were made, especially in Missiology and Homiletics, and Contemporary Theology was introduced

DIPLOMA COURSE, 1992

Old Testament

Old Testament Introduction

Old Testament English Exegesis

Old Testament Hebrew Grammar

Old Testament Hebrew Text

New Testament

New Testament Introduction

New Tetament English Exegesis

New Testament Greek Grammar

New Testament Greek Text

Church History

Early Church History
The Reformation
Puritanism and Evangelicalism
The Nineteenth Century
Nonconformity in Wales

Theology

Systematic Theology
Contemporary Theology

Missiology

The Bible, Theology and Mission
History of Missions
World Religions
Middle East Churches
Contemporary Movements

Pastoral Studies

Pastoral Theology
Homiletics

BA HONOURS DEGREE IN THEOLOGICAL STUDIES, 1993
YEAR 1

Strand 1 Biblical Studies	*Strand 2* Theological/Historical	*Strand 3* Applied Studies
Semester 1		
Hebrew Grammar	Church History/ Early Period	Biblical and Historical Perspectives/Preaching Pastoral Theology
Greek Grammar Textual Tools	God and His Word 20th Century Ecumenism/ Evangelical Resurgence	
Pentateuchal Studies Johannine Pet./Ep		
Semester 2		
Hebrew Grammar Greek Grammar OT Prophecy	Reformation God/Man Apologetics	Biblical Theology of Mission/Judaism Professional Placement

YEAR 2

Strand 1	*Strand 2*	*Strand 3*
Biblical Studies	Theological / Historical	Applied Studies

Semester 1

Hebrew Text	Puritanism	Social Action
Greek Text	Christology	Church Growth
		Contextualization
Pauline Studies	Charismatic and House Church Movements	Hinduism / Buddhism
OT / Isaiah, English		

Semester 2

Hebrew Text	19th Century Church Issues	Islam
Greek Text	Redemption	Christian Ministry
Psalms / Wisdom Lit. / NT Romans, English	Existentialist Phil.	Professional Placement

YEAR 3

Semester 1

Hebrew Text, Amos	Reformation and Separation	Preaching
OT Themes	Ecclesiology	Primal Religions
NT Hebrews	Existence of God:	Evangelism / Church
English	Arguments	Planting

Semester 2

OT Job / English	History and Theology of Revival	Pastoral Principles and Practice
NT 1 Cor. Greek	Eschatology	Medical Ethics
NT Pet / Pauline	Trends in Post-Modern Theology	New Religious Movements
Studies in Acts		

The course is arranged so that students have to take one strand from each module per semester, and have to take ten modules during one year. In the third year, the students have a choice of taking five modules in each semester, or four each, plus a dissertation, which corresponds to two modules. This provision gives the student a general knowledge and the opportunity to concentrate on a subject of special interest. There is, also, a system of prerequisites, governing progression from one year to the other.

C. STAFF, COUNCIL MEMBERS AND OFFICERS

STAFF/VISITING/PART-TIME LECTURERS

1936–1960

Rev. B. S. Fidler, Principal, **1936–60**

Rev. Glyndwr Davies, **1936/37–69** (continued after **1960**)

Rev. Ivor Powell, Princes Street, Barry

Rev. W. H. Hughes, Penarth, **1937–55**

Rev. F. J. Legge, Cardiff, **1938**

Rev. Victor Thomas, Aberdare, **1939**

Rev. W. E. Dalling, Sidmouth, Vice-Principal, **1944**

Rev. Rutt, Bristol, **1946**

Rev. F. S. Copleston, **1948–54, 1956–8**

Rev. Robert Rowland, **1948**

Rev. A. F. C. Read, **1948–51**

Rev. Omri Jenkins, Barry, **1951–63** (continued after **1960**)

Rev. Paul Tucker, **1954–5**

Rev. J. R. Morgan, Treharris, **1954–60**

Rev. Glyn Prosser, BA, Cardiff, **1954–6**

Rev. W. J. Crispus Jones, Ely, Cardiff, **1956**

Rev. Ken Peel, Princes Street, Barry, **1957**

A number of persons taught English, including George Cole, Mr Todd and Mrs Paul Tucker. For a brief period Mr J. Hatten was a visiting lecturer. From 1939 to 1942 Jim McHaffie was responsible for the Bible House and was regarded as a member of staff.

1960-1985

1960, Rev. J. C. J. Waite elected Principal and the Rev John Dart as Vice-Principal, but acted as Principal **1960–1**. John Waite, Principal until **1985**, John Dart, Vice-Principal until **1974**

Rev. D. C. C. Watson, **1964–6**

Rev. John Cook, **1966**, continued in Bryntirion, left **1991**

Rev. Noel Gibbard, **1978**, continued in Bryntirion

Visiting lecturers

Rev. Gerald Smith, Maesycwmer, **1960–6**

Rev. Derek Swann, Pontnewydd, Gwent, **1960–2**

Rev. John Thomas, Sandfields, Aberavon, **1960–9**

Rev. Emlyn Jones, Neath, **1960-**

Rev. Hugh D. Morgan, Newport, **1969–89**

Rev. Hubert Clement, Tonypandy, continued in Bryntirion

Rev. Noel Gibbard, Bynea, Llanelli, **1974**, full-time **1978**

Rev. Bernard Ward, Cardiff, **1976–7**

1985: Full-time

Rev. Eryl Davies, MA, BD, Ph.D, **1985**, Senior Tutor, **1987**, Principal
Rev. John Cook, BA, BD, from Barry, left **1991**
Rev. Noel Gibbard, MA, BD, Ph.D, from Barry
Rev. Iwan Rhys Jones, BA, BD, **1990**
Rev. Trevor Burke, BA, **1991–3**
Rev. Tom Holland, BD, part-time **1991**, full-time **1993**
Dr Tom Gledhill, **1993**
Miss Elvira Henry, Teacher of English

Part-time tutors

Mr John Sieczko, part-time **1986**, full-time **1987–90**
Mr Yasir Matloub, Cardiff
Rev. Paul Gardner, Northwich, Cheshire
Mr John Kendall, part-time tutor and Church pastoral worker
Mr Colin Nicholas, UK Director, WEC International
Rev. John Ross, Director, CWI
Rev. Peter Milsom, Pastor, Malpas Road, Newport
Rev. Malcolm Jones, Pastor, Maesycwmer
Rev. Sulwyn Jones, Pastor, Dowlais
Rev. Andrew Davies, Pastor, Bridgend
Dr David Cook, Director, Whitefield Institute, Oxford, and Fellow of
    Green College, Oxford
Rev. Stuart Olyott, Pastor, Belvidere, Liverpool
Dr Brian Harris, Consultant Psychiatrist and Senior Lecturer in Psych-
    iatry at University of Wales College of Medicine
Dr Karl Venn, General Medical Practitioner, Ebbw Vale, Gwent
Dr Dewi Arwel Hughes, Theological Consultant to Tear Fund
Dr Eddy Muskus, Spanish Gospel Mission, Zaragoza

Missionary Consultants, 1987-1991

Wolfgang Stumpf (RSMT), Colin Nicholas (WEC International), John
Wallis (OMF), Bob Cotton (EMF), Rob Rowley (SIM), Maurice Wheately
(AIM), Josef Tson (RMS)

Official College Representative in Romania and Asia

Jong Tae Lee

COUNCIL MEMBERS

College Council from 1940

1940

Rev. B. S. Fidler, MRST, BSE

Mrs Fidler

Miss B. M. Stephens, Tyla Morris, Pentyrch, Cardiff

T. K. Jenkins, Esq., 23 Rhydelyg Avenue, Cardiff

Rev. Victor Thomas, 13 Cemetery Road, Aberdare

Rev. F. J. Legge, 3 Old Penybryn, North Road, Cardiff; Upper Cliff House, Penarth

Rev. G. Davies, Baptist Manse, Beaufort; 8 Vaynor Street, Porth, Rhondda

Rev. J. McHaffie

1944

Rev. F. S. Copleston, 8 Vaynor Street, Porth, Rhondda

Rev. W. E. Dalling and Mrs Dalling

1945

Rev. J. W. Owen, Penryn, 2 Allensbank Road, Cardiff

Rev. D. C. Rowlands, 23 Clarke Street, Treorchy

T. L. Loveridge, Esq., 3 Hannah Street, Cardiff

E. Willie, Esq., 99 Westville Road, Cardiff

Mrs J. Powell, 13 Canon Street, Barry

Rev. R. Rowlands, Caenant Melyn, Hay; 7 Brentry Road and then 73 Thingwall Park, Bristol

1948

Rev. F. A. C. Read and Mrs Read

Miss M. Taylor

1950

Rev. Paul Tucker, 4 Ivor Street, Barry Island; 63, Oxford Street, Barry

1951

Rev. Omri Jenkins, Baptist Manse, Beryl Road, Barry

1954

Rev. J. R. Morgan, Oakleigh, Treharris

1955

Rev. Glyn Prosser, 21 Avondale Crescent, Grangetown, Cardiff

Mrs Paul Tucker

1956

Rev. J. Crispus Jones, BA, BD, Ely, Cardiff

Rev. Ken Peel, Princes Street, Barry

The following continued from September 1959, when the Executive
Council was formed, Rev. and Mrs Fidler, Mr T. Lawton Loveridge, Mr
and Mrs T. K. Jenkins, Miss B. M. Stephens, Rev. J. R. Morgan, Rev. Crispus
Jones, Rev. Ken Peel and the Rev. D. C. Rowlands

1960 Rev. Paul Tucker
          Rev. Omri Jenkins
          Rev. J. C. J. Waite, BD, Principal
          Rev. John Dart, MA, Vice-Principal

1962 Mr Ernest Lloyd, British
          Jews Society; CWI

1963 Mr John Capper, JP, Newport
          Rev. W. H. Parsons, Bath
          Dr Ken Barker, Pontardawe

1964 Rev. R. G. Tucker, Bath
          Mr B.L. Williams, Barry

1968 Professor Peter Gray, Cardiff
          Mr Maurice Garton, Newport

1974 Mr Clem Roberts, Barry

1975 Rev. Jim Cannon, Aber-big,

1977 Rev. Hugh D. Morgan,
          Newport, Rev. Maurice
          Wade, London

1978 Rev. Jim Webber, Newbridge

1979 Rev. Derek Swann,
          Pontnewydd

Bryntirion, 1983–1985

The Barry Council:

Revs Paul Tucker, John Dart, Jim Cannon, Hugh D. Morgan, Maurice
Wade, Jim Webber, Derek Swann, Messrs Ernest Lloyd, Ken Barker,
Clem Roberts and Maurice Garton (only eleven names included in Council
Minutes, while there should be twelve)

The Barry Council was joined by twelve *EMW representatives:*

Revs. J. Elwyn Davies, Eryl Davies, Sulwyn Jones, Peter Milsom, Neville
Rees, Gwynn Williams, Derek Garwood, Andrew Davies, Gareth Davies,
Arthur Pritchard, Bruce Powell and Gwilym Roberts

1985 Mr Anthony Gwyther-Jones

1989 Mr Ronnie Duke, Northern Ireland
          Mr Robert Davies, Abergavenny
          Rev. Dennis Jenkins, Llanelli
          Mr Wyn Thomas, Bangor

1990 Rev. Malcolm Laver, FIEC
          Rev. Alan Tovey, EFCC

1991 Mr Alastair Denton, Cardiff; Student representative appointed

PRESIDENT OF THE SCHOOL/COLLEGE

-1940	Mr Courcy Hamilton, St. Nicholas
1950	Rev. J. W. Owen, Heath, Cardiff
1963–5	Mr T. Lawton Loveridge, Penarth
1966–8	Mr John Capper, Newport
1983	Rev. J. Elwyn Davies, Port Talbot and Cwmafan

CHAIRMAN OF COUNCIL

1940–5	Rev. B. S. Fidler
1945–50	Rev. J. W. Owen, Cardiff
1950–63	Mr T. Lawton Loveridge
1963–85	Rev. Paul Tucker; the Barry Executive Council continued to meet until 4 July 1985
1983–7	Rev. Hugh D. Morgan, Newport, Council of the Evangelical Theological College of Wales; Vice-chairman, Rev. John Dart
1987	Dr Ken Barker, Pontardawe; Vice-chairman, Rev. Gwilym Roberts

SECRETARY

	George Cole
1940–50	Rev. J. McHaffie—new Council, but had acted as secretary, **1938-9**
1950–5	Rev.Paul Tucker
1955–6	Rev. Glyn Prosser
1957–75	Rev. Ken Peel
1976–83	Rev. Jim Cannon
1983	Mr Maurice Garton

TREASURER

	Mr Jesse Hatten
1940–55	Mr T. Knight Jenkins
1955–81	Miss B. M. Stephens
1981–5	Rev. Maurice Wade
1985–7	Mr Anthony Gwyther-Jones
1985–90	Rev. Maurice Wade, Financial Secretary

ACCOUNTANT

	Mr Reg Hayes, Cardiff
1991	Mr Alastair Denton, Cardiff

WARDEN/CATERER/MATRON

1936–59	Mrs Fidler with help from others, e.g., **1936-8**, Mrs Blid;
1948–51	Mrs Read
1960	Mr and Mrs John Jones
1962–73	Mr and Mrs Lord, with help from Mrs Waite, Mrs Dart, Mr and Mrs Whiting
1973–85	Trevor and Catherine Macey, continuing help from Mr and Mrs Whiting, and Mrs Cook helped for one period
1985	Mr and Mrs Howard Davies
1988	Mr and Mrs Kelvin Olsen-Vetland; from **1994** employed by the College. John Lang, assistant warden
1994	Miss Iola Thomas, Accommodations Officer/Matron

OFFICE SECRETARY

Before **1960** a number of different people helped, including Miss M. Taylor=Mrs Selway

1960–85	Mrs Ardley, Mrs Pritchard, Mrs Lorna Waite

From **1985**:

1985–6	Miss Ann Matthews, Bridgend
1987–	Mrs Chris Connor, Cardiff
1990–4	Miss Shân Carter, Bridgend
1994–	Miss Valérie Fanguin, France

Index